D097126D

In business for 42 years, I have never found a substitute for diligence and hard work. In *A Man's Guide to Work*, Pat Morley captures the work ethic in an exciting application plan that can change your life forever!

ED "SKIP" AST
Chairman and CEO of Shasta Industries

So many people separate their spiritual lives from their vocational lives. It's a huge mistake, and Pat Morley has addressed that issue head-on. He has developed a theology of work that is an essential topic for every man and woman whose full-time ministry is right where they are. Pat is a good friend, a tremendous communicator, and an authentic disciple of Christ.

RON BLUE, President
Kingdom Advisors

I would crumble to pieces if not for doing the "works prepared beforehand for us to walk in" that Paul describes in Ephesians 2:10. Work is the psychological glue that holds a man together. And who better to develop a practical contemporary "theology of work" than Pat Morley. It is at the very center of effective leadership.

BOB BUFORD
Founding Chairman, Leadership Network
Author, *Halftime* and *Finishing Well*
(Bob's next book, *Musings for Friends*, is free at bobbuford.com.)

Breaking news: God wants your work, whatever it is, to be your ministry! Stay tuned to hear how Patrick Morley's *A Man's Guide to Work: 12 Ways to Honor God on the Job*, will help you transform your work on Monday to an act of worship!

DAN CATHY
President and Chief Operating Officer
Chick-fil-A, Inc.
Atlanta, Georgia

I love *A Man's Guide To Work*. I'm going to work through it with my two sons. This book will rival *The Man In The Mirror*. Pat's experience as both businessman and seminary graduate puts him in a unique position to teach us a biblical theology of work. *A Man's Guide To Work* will empower you to find fulfillment, joy, and satisfaction in your work!

JAMES W. HEAVENER
Co-chairman/CEO
Full Sail University

This book is long overdue! As men we devote half our waking hours to work, yet hear very little—if anything—about a "theology of work." As a business-man, I'm always looking for one-of-a-kind investments that produce a steady, ongoing return. Pat's book *A Man's Guide to Work* is just such an investment. Read it. Apply it. It will change your life!

> H. WAYNE HUIZENGA JR
> President, Huizenga Holdings

This really is "The Perfect Storm"! Men . . . Work . . . and Pat Morley! Pat's incredible heart for men, coupled with his biblical worldview on business, make this a must read for any man who hungers for a work life full of purpose and impact. What a great moment for Pat Morley to again step into our lives with *A Man's Guide to Work.*

> DOUG HUNTER
> President and CEO
> Fellowship of Companies for Christ International/Christ@Work

When I became a Christian, I had no idea how God would want me to run a business. I wish Pat Morley had written *A Man's Guide to Work* 30 years ago. Many of the lessons I learned the hard way you can learn by simply reading this book. There are no shortcuts, but having the right information can make your journey a lot easier.

> NORM MILLER
> Chairman, Interstate Batteries

Patrick Morley has truly captured the compelling reasons why we go to work. This book grabbed my heart. The Holy Spirit has prompted him to show us how God can use the workplace to forge our lives and impact the lives of those around us.

> PATRICK O'NEAL, President, Chatham Development Corp.,
> former National Executive Director, CBMC

You will find this powerful faith—and values-based approach to work a great read. It's totally consistent with what we're trying to teach our students—plus adds the faith component. I highly recommend it.

> STEVE REINEMUND
> Dean of Business
> Wake Forest University
> Schools of Business
> Retired Chairman/CEO—PepsiCo

A MAN'S GUIDE TO
WORK

12 WAYS TO HONOR GOD ON THE JOB

PATRICK MORLEY

MOODY PUBLISHERS
CHICAGO

Editor: Jim Vincent
Interior Design: Smartt Guys design
Cover Design: Brand Navigation, LLC
Cover Images: istock 6918572, istock 5533371, istock 6244000

All websites and phone numbers listed herein are accurate at the time of publication, but may change in the future or cease to exist. The listing of website references and resources does not imply publisher endorsement of the site's entire contents. Groups and organizations are listed for informational purposes, and listing does not imply publisher endorsement of their activities.

Library of Congress Cataloging-in-Publication Data

Morley, Patrick M.
   A man's guide to work : 12 ways to honor God on the job / Patrick Morley.
      p. cm.
   Includes bibliographical references.
   ISBN 978-0-8024-7554-1
   1. Work—Religious aspects—Christianity. 2. Men—Religious life. I. Title.

BT738.5.M67 2010
248.8'8—dc22

2009033801

We hope you enjoy this book from Moody Publishers. Our goal is to provide high-quality, thought-provoking books and products that connect truth to your real needs and challenges. For more information on other books and products written and produced from a biblical perspective, go to www.moodypublishers.com or write to:

Moody Publishers
820 N. LaSalle Boulevard
Chicago, IL 60610

1 3 5 7 9 10 8 6 4 2

Printed in the United States of America

In Memory of
Scott Alexander
1955–2009

He could easily have become a famous recording artist and a hero to your kids. Instead, he decided to stay home and become a hero to his own kids. For two decades Scott owned a business in Orlando where he developed a fine reputation which, in turn, opened many doors for him to bring glory to God. Scott used to travel with me and sing at our men's events.

Scott was a great husband, father, and friend, and we all miss him deeply.

Contents

Introduction

YOU WERE CREATED TO WORK, and you will feel most happy, most alive, and most useful when you are doing the work you were created to do. The act of productivity is its own reward.

This is a book for men in the workplace—men who want to integrate their faith and work. You may be a businessman, construction worker, salesman, entrepreneur, lawyer, prison guard, accountant, plumber, nurse, or doctor. You may work in commerce, health care, manufacturing, education, the military, technology, the arts, the judicial system, or public safety.

Whatever your work is, you want to—as Apple founder Steve Jobs likes to say—leave a dent in the universe. You want it to matter that you have walked across the face of this planet. You don't want to end up as another notch on the belt of history. You don't want to merely be a shooting star that streaked across the sky one night, then disappeared. You want your life to count, to make a difference. I would like to show you how you can do that.

Unfortunately, over 50 percent of all workers are dissatisfied[1] with their jobs—a record high—and as many as 80 percent are not in jobs best suited for them.[2] That's tragic, since about half of your 112 waking hours each week will be devoted to work and your work commute.

Most men do not have what we might call "a theology of work." They feel theologically stranded—left to cobble together their own doctrine of work. They have not been trained for the marketplace. Ask most Christian men, "Is business or plumbing a calling, like being a pastor? What is God's purpose for you in the marketplace?" or a dozen similar questions, and you will probably get blank stares. That's not because the Bible is thin on the subject. Far from it. The Bible is replete with wisdom for every work situation you will ever encounter.

My passion is men's discipleship, and I write books. Given that half of a man's life is bound up in his work, that alone is enough motivation for me to teach you on the subject. But there are other reasons for me to write. I have the unusual distinction of being trained in both business and theology. I am a seminary graduate, but I am first and foremost a businessman. In fact, I have been the president or managing partner of fifty-nine companies and partnerships. I have a PhD in management, specializing in leadership and organizational change. I've been through many business cycles. And I spent seven years successfully fighting off bankruptcy—very humbling.

I tell you these things because I want you to know that I am not writing from the bleachers. I've been on the battlefield too, and I know what you're going through day by day. In this book I consider it my privilege and duty to share with you what the Bible teaches as a theology of work.

Whether you are new to Christian faith but experienced in work, or new to work but experienced in Christian faith, here's my promise. By the end of this book, I will have shown you how to experience the power of God in your work. You will learn how to bring about social transformation through your work. And I will show you how you can make your work life count for the glory of God.

How to Use This Book

You can, of course, read this book in the normal way. However, I would encourage you to study the book with a group of men. At the end of each chapter you will find "Questions for Personal Reflection or Group Discussion" for that purpose. You could meet for one hour each week and discuss a chapter. You can also use the book in conjunction with the "Doing Business God's Way" Bible study series available at no cost in video or audio at http://www.maninthemirror.org/biblestudy/series.htm.

Okay, let's go to work, shall we? First, let's explore your calling as a man in the workforce.

CALLING:

BUSINESSMAN, Plumber, or Minister—SAME THING

MEN WHO FOLLOW JESUS CHRIST are an occupation force "ordained" to serve in the markets of men. We should regard work not just as a platform for ministry—work *is* ministry, and we are stewards put in charge until Jesus comes back, a fifth column who infiltrate a world stained by sin, acting as salt that preserves the way of Christ and light that leads broken people out of darkness. We are liberators sent to free a world that labors under the groan of sin, ambassadors sent "into" the world (which at the same time we are not part "of"), taking risks to build Christ's kingdom while not neglecting to tend earth's culture. We are workers doing our part as God sovereignly orchestrates "the main thing"—to bring people into right relationship with Him and right relationship with each other.

Same Work, Two Results

Picture two airline ticket agents. They do exactly the same job, but one views his work as something he does to earn money, so when he finishes his shift, he can do what he really wants to do. He is easily irritated by customers complaining when their travel plans go awry.

The second agent views his work as a calling. Every time someone comes to him with a problem, he sees it as an opportunity to serve the customer and represent his great God. The agent does what he was called to do to the glory of God, even when facing resistance from a particular customer.

That second ticket agent understands the big idea that undergirds this chapter: Whether you're a businessman or a minister, your work is a calling. It has intrinsic value, and it has potential to bear eternal fruit that honors God.

To Work Is Part of God's Nature—and Ours

Work is part of God's nature and character. John 5:17 portrays both the Father and Jesus as workers. Jesus said, "My father is always at his work to this very day, and I, too, am working."

Psalm 8 offers a glimpse into how God incorporated work into our nature too. The psalmist writes, "When I consider your heavens, the work of your fingers, the moon and the stars, which you have set in place, what is man that you are mindful of him, the son of man that you care for him?" (vv. 3–4).

The question gets answered two ways. First, he describes our *identity*—who God created us to be: "You made him a little lower than the heavenly beings and crowned him with glory and honor" (v. 5).

And then he describes our *purpose*—what God created us to do: "You made [man] ruler over the works of your hands; you put everything under his feet" (v. 6).

God has dominion over the whole earth and all of creation—a dominion that He has delegated to us.

Work, it turns out, is part of our nature and character too. We have been created to work, and you will never find complete peace on earth until you discover what God has called you to do. Sadly, many workers have not—some surveys have shown that up to 80 percent of people are not in jobs best suited for them.

Is Work a Blessing or a Curse?

It's comforting to know we were created to work, but is work a blessing or a curse? Many assume that work is part of the curse that resulted from Adam and Eve's sin—what we commonly call "the fall." As a result of that sin, God told Adam, "Cursed is the ground because of you; through painful toil you will eat of it all the days of your life. It will produce thorns and thistles for you, and you will eat the plants of the field. By the sweat of your brow you will eat your food until you return to the ground" (Genesis 3:17–19).

Ouch! But work itself was created prior to the fall in Genesis 2 as a blessing from God, not in Genesis 3 where, because of the fall, work was made difficult.

From day one, man was commissioned to work. After creating the world, the earth became lush with vegetation—and there was a garden. When God created Adam, He gave him a task: "The Lord God took the man and put him in the Garden of Eden to work it and take care of it" (Genesis 2:15). And that was before the fall, so work has both a blessing and a curse.

> *A MAN WILL FEEL MOST USEFUL AND HAPPY WHEN HE IS DOING WHAT GOD CREATED HIM TO DO.*

Work has a blessing because we are created in such a way that a man will feel most alive, most useful, and most happy when he is doing what he was created to do.

A man who is happy in his work is happy indeed. But a man who is unhappy in his work will be unhappy everywhere. In fact, most men can be unhappy at home and still find happiness if their work is satisfying. That's not so surprising given that almost half your time—and most of your intellectual energy—is devoted to work.

Work also has a curse on it because of the fall. In business, if you pick the wrong strategy, your effort is going to be . . . what? A lot of hard work. But if you pick the right strategy, your effort is going to be . . . what? A lot of hard work. Whether you pick the right or the wrong strategy, because of the fall your efforts are going to be a lot of hard work. Because of the fall, *we must do our work while feeling the prick of thorns.*

Is a Career in Ministry More Spiritual than a Career in Business?

Once I visited a church in my hometown. For about forty minutes, the guest preacher said, in essence, that if you really love Jesus, you will go to the mission field. When the service was over, I slinked out of the sanctuary. I felt that if I didn't become a full-time career missionary, I always would be a second-class citizen in God's kingdom.

That distorted view, severing our work life from our spiritual life, is biblically inaccurate. It's not at all in alignment with God's intention related to our work. From a scriptural viewpoint, it's utter fiction.

For those who live under this distortion, secular jobs have eternal value only when we use them as a "platform for ministry." These people go through the day counting the minutes till the next coffee break, so they can ask their coworkers about their spiritual lives. They can't wait for the workday to be over. They can't see that the work itself has inherent spiritual value.

Of course, God's kingdom does have a global mandate—a command to Jesus' followers to take the gospel throughout the world, and to grow His kingdom in every culture on earth. But that's hardly the only thing we are commanded to do.

God calls us to "build the kingdom" and "tend the culture." That's the Great Commission and the Cultural Mandate. Building the kingdom is the Great Commission: "Go and make disciples . . ." (see Matthew 28:19–20). Tending the culture—which occupies the vast majority of our time—is the Cultural Mandate: God created mankind in His own image, blessed them, and sent them to fill and subdue the earth, and rule over the fish, the birds, and every living thing (Genesis 1:27–28).

The Cultural Mandate includes our roles in families, communities, government, education, health care, the arts, law, science, the trades, and commerce. Work is part of the Cultural Mandate.

Both the Great Commission and the Cultural Mandate are high and holy callings.

Work, it turns out, can be a calling just like going into the ministry. Every vocation is holy to the Lord. God makes no distinction between sacred and secular. If you look up the word *secular* in your Bible concordance, what will you find? Nothing, because the word *secular* is not in the Bible. Twentieth-century evangelical theologian and philosopher Francis Schaeffer, in answering practical questions written to him by everyday people, noted, "One thing you should very definitely have in mind—that is that a ministry such as teaching the Bible in a college is no higher calling intrinsically than being a businessman or doing something else."[1]

God calls some people to be pastors or teachers or evangelists. And He calls some to work in businesses, hospitals, fire departments, or construction.

You Are an "Ordained" Worker

I remember a man who once visited the Friday morning Man in the Mirror Bible study I lead, who told me, "All my life I wanted to be a high school math teacher. Finally, my dream came true. But I soon saw two problems. First, my students were coming to class with problems math can't solve. Second, the Christian teachers in my school don't know each other. God has put a vision in my mind about how to address those two issues. I am an ordained math teacher."

He sure got that right. If you are a Christian in the marketplace—whether driving the truck, fixing the computers, or running the company—you are "ordained" to that position.

In his book *The Call*, Christian thinker Os Guinness quotes some poignant thoughts from great thinkers and saints about the holiness of all vocations. Here are some of them:

- Martin Luther, a German theologian credited with initiating the Protestant Reformation, wrote this: "The works of monks and priests, however holy and arduous [they] may be, do not differ one whit in the sight of God from the works of the rustic laborer in the field or the woman going about her household tasks."
- William Tyndale, a Protestant reformer and scholar of the sixteenth century who translated the Bible into the early modern English of his day, wrote, "If our desire is to please God, pouring water, washing dishes, cobbling shoes, and preaching the Word is all one."
- Abraham Kuyper, a Dutch theologian, journalist, statesman, and politician who served as prime minister of the Netherlands (1901–1905), said, "There is not one square inch of the entire creation about which Jesus Christ would not cry out 'This is mine, this belongs to me.'"

- William Perkins, a clergyman and Cambridge theologian who also was one of the foremost leaders of the Puritan movement in the Church of England, claimed, "Polishing shoes is a sanctified and holy act." He added, "The action of a shepherd in keeping sheep performed as I have said it, is as good a work before God as is the action of a judge giving sentence. Or of a magistrate in ruling. Or a minister in preaching."
- Bishop Thomas Beacon wrote, "Our Savior Christ was a carpenter, his apostles were fishermen. St. Paul was a tent maker."[2]

These statements support our "big idea" for this chapter: Regardless of whether you're a businessman or a minister, your work is a calling—a task given by God. When we see our daily work in that light, we understand that God assigns meaning and dignity to what we do at work.

Work *Is* Ministry

As we noted in the first paragraph, work is *not* just a platform to do ministry— it *is* ministry. If you are a waiter, every couple sitting at your station is a divine appointment. They provide an opportunity for you to serve them in the name of Jesus Christ. "How may I help you?" "May I take your order?"

If you are a salesman, every appointment is holy, and every closing is sacred.

If you are a manager, every time you intervene between two employees who cannot see eye-to-eye, you have an opportunity to demonstrate the reconciling power of the gospel of Jesus Christ.

Obviously, some things are sinful. As Christians, we do not have freedom to participate in careers or jobs that require those activities. But everything else is spiritual. Schaeffer put it this way:

> There are certain things which are given as absolutely sinful in the Scripture, and these things we as Christians should not do. . . . But then everything else is spiritual. The painting of a picture, the work of a good shoemaker, the doctor, the lawyer—all these things are spiritual if they are done within the circle of what is taught in Scripture, looking to the Lord day by day for His help.[3]

The landscape designer, the building contractor, the UPS deliveryman, the chief executive officer—all of these people have chosen employment that can be spiritual when accomplished within the circle drawn by Scripture. Every vocation can be holy to the Lord, if we look to Him day by day for His help. For the Christian, all of life is "spiritual."

Work Should Bring Glory to God

Your occupation is part of your call to service. Faith is not a private thing to be kept in a compartment. Instead, on the job your faith should season every action and word so that God will receive praise, glory, and honor. What does that look like in action? The apostle Paul gives us some key clues in 1 Thessalonians 4:11–12, writing, "Make it your ambition to lead a quiet life, to mind your own business and to work with your hands, just as we told you, so that your daily life may win the respect of outsiders and so that you will not be dependent on anybody."

Not everything you do has to result in someone's immediate salvation. Just working in a way that wins the respect of other people is valuable to God's kingdom. And furthermore, it is valuable to work in such a way that you limit your dependence on other people (e.g., not going into debt). Those simple aspects of living out your calling will enhance God's reputation in our culture.

The New Testament has a lot to say about the nature and value of work. Paul wrote, "For even when we were with you, we gave you this rule: 'If a man will not work, he shall not eat'" (2 Thessalonians 3:10). That's easy to understand. Some people resist working—it can be uncomfortable and tiring and demanding, especially now that we feel the prick of the thorns

> *YOUR WORK HAS INTRINSIC VALUE AND THE POTENTIAL TO BEAR ETERNAL FRUIT.*

described in Genesis 3:18. But Paul said if a capable person doesn't work, then you shouldn't give him anything to eat. Work is a scriptural mandate—a commandment.

The Scripture tells us, "So whether you eat or drink or whatever you do, do it all for the glory of God" (1 Corinthians 10:31). Most of us can accept that work is a command. But this verse implies that, no matter what your job is, you can do it for God's glory.

Simply put, your work is a summons to follow Jesus. Your work enables you to go where Jesus would go, to be what Jesus would be, and to do what Jesus would do. That is a calling. We will experience resistance—that's part of the curse. But when we see work as a calling, we know we can do it for God's glory.

Work is a noble and holy vocation. That's the "big idea" for this chapter: Regardless of whether you're a businessman or a minister, your work is a calling. It has intrinsic value, and it has potential to bear eternal fruit.

Staying Where You Are

Many men who sense the desire to serve God welling up within them assume they must now do something else. This is rarely the case. Instead, God wants them to use their talents where they are, reaching others with the gospel and influencing the culture in the process. That's what Norm Miller, chairman of Interstate Batteries, did.

Norm Miller went to work at Interstate Batteries more than four decades ago, at the age of twenty-four. Eight years later Norm received Jesus Christ as his Lord and Savior. Norm prayed, "God, I will do anything You want me to do." But he didn't sense a calling to leave his job. He said, "I didn't know anything but batteries, so I just decided to stay in batteries."

He began rising in that growing company and eventually became the CEO. In 1976, for the first time in its history, Interstate Batteries sold one million batteries in a single year. Today, his company now sells fourteen million batteries per year. Would that have happened if Norm had left? Maybe, but we know for sure it did happen, at least partly, because he was willing to stay right where God had called him. And because he stayed, he has had tremendous opportunity to use the platform God gave him to influence our culture. He's made a profound difference, because he answered God's call and understood his purpose in business.

You might think that going from a million batteries to fourteen million batteries is some kind of overnight, superstar performance. But I ran the math, and what it comes down to is an annualized growth rate of 8.5 percent. That requires the perseverance of steady plodding over the long haul.

For most of us, our calling probably is to stay right where we are, but to change the way we see our jobs. The apostle Paul said, "Each one should retain the place in life that the Lord assigned to him and to which God has called him." And a few verses later he reiterated, "Each man, as responsible to God, should remain in the situation God called him to" (1 Corinthians 7:17, 24). Many of us will find we can increase our impact simply by staying where we are with a new perspective that our vocation is holy to the Lord.

Going Into Ministry Is No Panacea

When I stepped away from day-to-day business to devote myself "full time" to the ministry of helping men think more deeply about their lives, I thought I would wake up the next day feeling more spiritual—somehow "holier." It never happened.

Then I supposed that when I looked into the mirror, I would see the faint outline of a halo. Oh, I didn't think anyone else would ever see it, but I thought for sure that I would. It never happened.

I thought my walk with Christ would soar to new heights since I was now working "directly" for Him all day. It never happened.

Actually, I feel no more "called" to writing, speaking, and teaching than I did to developing buildings. I am no more passionate about what I do now than about what I did before. Don't get me wrong—I'm very passionate. But I was also very passionate about developing real estate.

Climbing the Ladder

Do you have to be a superstar? Do you have to have five talents? Do you have to have the big bucks? Most of us will never be in that category. But we all can increase our impact, even while we stay right where God has planted us. Stay focused on God's mandate: "You're in charge until I get back."

In his book *Business as a Calling*, Michael Novak explains,

Being a middle manager is not primarily a way station on the way to the top. Probably everyone at first wants to test themselves against that possibility, but realistically most middle managers expect some advancement over a lifetime, higher salaries and bonuses, and most of all, the ever-higher respect of their peers; while remaining middle managers until retirement. Middle management, many know early, is their calling; they want to be super good at it. They want to make a contribution. Most of all, they need to know in their own minds that they have done so.[4]

God tells us, "You're in charge until I get back." But that doesn't necessarily mean we're supposed to strive to be the top guy. We can't all be CEOs.

Changing Jobs

But what if, like many men, you just don't like your work?

Viktor Frankl, who survived the horrors of Auschwitz to become a famous psychotherapist, is best known for saying, "A man's search for meaning is the primary motivation of his life."[5]

Once in Vienna, a diplomat came to see him. The man was depressed about his work. Frankl discovered the man did not like his job with the U.S. government. The man had been in psychotherapy for five years, and his therapist had convinced him that his difficulties would end if he could reconcile his relationship with his authoritarian father. The therapist said the U.S. government was a father figure, so the man's current dissatisfaction resulted from unresolved issues from the past with his own dad.

After a few interviews, Frankl said, "It seems to me that you don't like what you do, and there is no reason to keep doing it. Why don't you get another job?" So the man did. Five years later, he reported he was a really happy person because he found something he loved to do.[6]

Practical Ideas If You Don't Know Your Calling

What if you are called to the marketplace but haven't found your niche? Or what if you're ready for a career change?

Many of us will not hold the same job for our entire career. We may even discover we missed our calling altogether, and we may change the entire focus of our work. That's certainly a valid response to a sense of dissatisfaction. To find your calling, consider four things: your natural motivated interests, natural abilities, acquired abilities, and spiritual gifts. Here are a few thoughts to get you started.

1. Where do your natural interests lie?

Edward Crosby Johnson first observed his grandfather, a missionary doctor. Then he watched his father, who worked in a family retailing business. He noticed that his father loved his hobbies but found no pleasure in his work. Johnson decided to find something he liked to do *and* was good at. He started out as a lawyer, but that didn't quite work out. In the 1940s he got a management contract for a small, start-up mutual fund called Fidelity, headquartered in Boston, Massachusetts.

Johnson loved his company, and over the years he built up Fidelity Investments to be a premier mutual fund company. According to Michael Novak's book *Business as a Calling*, Johnson wrote this to his Harvard classmates: "It is a real thrill to try to give the small investor, by which our company is mainly comprised, as good a job of investing as the big man gets." That thought gave his life meaning and purpose throughout his life as he increased the range of funds available to small investors.

What types of tasks interest and motivate you? Is it innovating, designing, selling, organizing, planning, working with your hands? What kinds of tasks do you enjoy?

What types of jobs interest you? Computer programmer, manager, accountant, salesman, owner? What kinds of jobs do you enjoy?

2. What are your natural abilities?

Another investor, John Templeton, started life wanting to be a missionary. Then, while he was at Oxford, he met some missionaries and realized he didn't have the right stuff to be a missionary. "But," he said, "I do have the ability to make money." So he devoted his life to making money to support missionaries.

What are your natural aptitudes and abilities? How has God designed your body and your brain? If you're five-feet-six-inches tall and can't dribble, you're not going to play for the Los Angeles Lakers, right? Similar principles apply to all types of employment. God made you in a certain way. So look at your natural assets. What are you good at? Do you like to work with numbers? It would be foolish to try to become a lawyer if you prefer to work with numbers. If you like to work with numbers but feel shy around people, you may be more suited to accounting than sales. What comes easily to you?

3. What are your acquired abilities?

Acquired abilities are the things you are trained to do. For the past several years, I've been racing sports cars. To help me get started, I hired a racing coach. If you knew him, you'd understand why he's good at his job. You can ask him any question about racing or mechanics, and he will know the answer. He didn't come into the world with all that knowledge embedded in his brain. Obviously, he has a natural ability to understand those things, but he acquired a high level of competency through study and experience. In the same way, you may have some acquired competency that would lead you into a work calling. It could be from formal education, on the job training, or even a hobby.

4. What are your spiritual abilities/gifts?

In the same way that we pursue vocational employment based upon our aptitudes and abilities, we can also look at how God has spiritually gifted us.

Every believer receives at least one spiritual gift. "Now to each one the manifestation of the Spirit is given for the common good" (1 Corinthians 12:7). The Holy Spirit determines our spiritual gifts. "Each man has his own gift from God . . . he gives them to each one, just as he determines" (1 Corinthians 7:7; 12:11).

The purpose of our spiritual gifts is to serve Christ by serving others. "Each one should use whatever gift he has received to serve others, faithfully administering God's grace in its various forms" (1 Peter 4:10).

These gifts usually synchronize to natural abilities. So knowing your spiritual gifts can help you be more effective in your calling.

While theologians and teachers often differ on how to precisely classify and name spiritual gifts, the following generally captures the gist of the different gifts:

1. *Service gifts.* Service gifts are often low-profile, behind-the-scenes gifts. They include showing mercy, service (or helps), hospitality, giving, administration, leadership, faith, and discernment.

2. *Speaking gifts.* Speaking gifts include knowledge, wisdom, preaching, teaching, evangelism, apostleship, shepherding, and encouragement.

3. *Signifying gifts.* The signifying gifts are miracles, healing, speaking in tongues, and the interpretation of tongues.

To better understand your gifts, you can study the four passages of Scripture that deal with spiritual gifts: Romans 12:3–8; 1 Corinthians 12:1–31; Ephesians 4:11–13; and 1 Peter 4:9–11. Prayerfully write down the gifts to which you are drawn.

For more, go to www.maninthemirror.org/alm/alm157.htm to read "How to Determine Your Spiritual Gifts," including one-sentence explanations of each spiritual gift.

So is there a sacred and a secular calling? In the biblical mind-set, there is no chasm between sacred and secular. Regardless of whether you're a businessman or a minister, your work is a calling. It has intrinsic value, and it has potential to bear eternal fruit.

A PRAYER YOU CAN PRAY

Lord Jesus, thank You for the clarity of Your Word regarding every issue in life. You have made the desire to work part of my nature—a nature that is made in Your image. Help me to find the vocation that best suits who You have created me to be. I know that I will feel most alive, most useful, and most happy when I am doing what I was created to do. Help me to bring You glory through my work—even as I feel the prick of thorns. Give me a renewed sense of commitment. Give me a broader perspective and a greater resolve to walk in Your way at work. Help me understand that whether I am in full-time "ministry" or work in the marketplace, it's all the same. It's a calling with eternal value and consequence. I pray this in Jesus' name, amen.

Questions for Personal Reflection
or Group Discussion

1. Have you felt like your work was a calling or not? Explain your answer.

2. Which of the following statements best summarizes how you have viewed work in the past, and why?
   - Spiritual jobs are more important than secular jobs
   - Work is a platform to do ministry
   - Work has intrinsic value and is equal to any other calling

3. What does the Bible say about work in Genesis 2:15; 3:17; Psalm 8:5–8; Ecclesiastes 2:24–26; and 2 Thessalonians 3:10? What are the implications for your view of work as a calling?

PURPOSE:

WHY Do We WORK?

I HAD A BUSINESS MEETING with two incredibly moral, ethical people. By the end of the meeting, it was clear they had three primary reasons for working—to earn a living, accumulate money, and be personally fulfilled.

They had an altogether different reason for being at that meeting than I did. My purpose for being there was to participate in the abundant life—to give, to serve, to receive God's blessings, and to bring glory to God by my actions.

They were limited to reaching the top of Maslow's hierarchy of needs (esteem and self-actualization needs). We were pursuing the same deal but for different reasons.

In this chapter, we will flesh out why the purpose of work for a Christian is different. The answer starts by understanding "the main thing."

The Main Thing That Is Always Happening

What is "the main thing" that God is always doing in the world? It's bringing people into right relationship with Him and right relationship with each other.

To achieve this God has established four universal purposes for us—two for relationships and two for tasks:

- The Great Commandment: To love God (Matthew 22:37)
- The New Commandment: To love one another (John 13:34)
- The Great Commission: To build the kingdom (Matthew 28:18–20)
- The Cultural Mandate: To tend the culture (Genesis 1:28)

This is what God wants to happen. This is God's agenda for us—His end game. But He doesn't leave it to human will or effort. Instead, He sovereignly oversees His plan and purpose (Romans 9:16).

GOD ORCHESTRATES ALL HUMAN EVENTS TO BRING PEOPLE INTO RIGHT RELATIONSHIP WITH HIMSELF.

"The main thing" always happening is that God sovereignly orchestrates all human events to bring people into right relationship with Himself and with each other.

So when something at work seems to randomly go right or wrong, it isn't random at all. It is God sovereignly orchestrating all human events—even the seemingly random circumstances—to bring you into (or keep you) in right relationship with Him and with other people.

The marketplace is the great arena of human events—innovating, manufacturing, building, buying, selling, serving customers, making markets. And the main thing happening in your work is that God is sovereignly orchestrating all the seemingly unrelated occurrences of your day to bring you—and the people you touch—into right relationship with Him and right relationship with people.

This is the ultimate purpose of work: to bring people into right relationship with God and with each other.

Once you see your work life the way God sees your work life, it is a perspective that will permeate every human encounter, every decision you make, and every minute you allocate.

The purpose of your work is to improve people's lives—to bring them into right relationship with God and others.

Stewards: "You're in Charge until I Get Back"

Jesus told a story (the parable of the talents in Matthew 25:14–30) about a wealthy man who was planning to leave for an extended trip. To ensure the care of his property while he was gone, he called his servants together and delegated responsibilities, according to their abilities. To the first servant, he gave sixty thousand dollars in today's money. To the second, he gave twenty-four thousand dollars. And to the last, he gave twelve thousand.

The first servant went right to work, and he doubled the money his master had entrusted to him. The second servant did the same. But the third servant—the one entrusted with the smallest investment—simply dug a hole and buried his master's money for safekeeping.

After a long absence, the master returned and asked for an accounting of his assets. The first and second servants showed how they had doubled the money he left with them. To both of them, the master responded, "Good work! You did your job well. From now on be my partner" (vv. 21, 23 MESSAGE).

Then it was time for the last servant to report. He said, "Master, I know you have high standards and hate careless ways, that you demand the best and make no allowances for error. I was afraid I might disappoint you, so I found a good hiding place and secured your money. Here it is, safe and sound down to the last cent" (v. 25 MESSAGE).

The master was furious, Jesus said:

> "That's a terrible way to live!" [the master said]. "It's criminal to live cautiously like that! If you knew I was after the best, why did you do less than the least? The least you could have done would have been to invest the sum with the bankers, where at least I would have gotten a little interest. Take [twelve] thousand and give it to the one who risked the most. And get rid of this 'play-it-safe' who won't go out on a limb. Throw him out into utter darkness." (vv. 26–30 MESSAGE)

God has entrusted His property—His creation—to us, His servants. Basically, He has said, "You're in charge until I get back." That's the big idea of this chapter. He has delegated dominion over His creation—the world—to us.

We each end up with different responsibilities based on our levels of ability. God's purpose is that we will use our talents and abilities to "occupy" the world—we are an occupation force called to alleviate suffering and establish His kingdom principles in our culture.

We Liberate People from "the Groan"

When I was eighteen, I quit high school in the middle of my senior year. My dad wasn't going to let me hang around the house, so he escorted me down to the army enlistment office. You can just imagine the issues that culminated in my becoming a dropout—and the horrible example it set for my three younger brothers. The emotional pain was intense for everyone.

Although I saw my family from time to time after that, I did not really reconnect with them—at least emotionally—until I was in my late twenties. That's when I started taking my father to lunch every year on his birthday, December 12.

We had done this for about five years when one day, as we left the restaurant, we discovered we were parked next to each other. He was getting into his truck to return to work, and I was going to my car. We stood near our vehicles, and I said, "Dad, I'd like to give you a hug."

I wrapped my arms around him, and as he hugged me back, my dad let out this primordial groan: "Uhhmmmmmmmm!" It lasted for at least twenty seconds. It was like a whole lifetime of frustration and dissatisfaction and weariness over "what might have been" was captured in that single moment. A century of sorrows boiled over.

By the time he stopped, I was weeping, and he was too. I said, "I love you, Dad." And he said, "I love you too." That was the first time I ever remember my Dad saying, "I love you."

You have something in your life that makes you want to groan as well. You are not alone. The Bible says that the whole world is groaning:

We know that the whole creation has been groaning as in the pains of childbirth right up to the present time. Not only so, but we ourselves, who have the firstfruits of the Spirit, groan inwardly as we wait eagerly for our adoption as sons. (Romans 8:22–23)

Creation groans. We groan. Because of sin, the things that should be easy are not. Work is difficult. God always intended that we would work, but now we must groan as we do our work while feeling the prick of thorns. But we also read that "the groan" exists for a good purpose:

> For the creation [including humans] was subjected to frustration [or futility], not by its own choice, but by the will of the one who subjected it [God], in hope that the creation itself will be liberated from its bondage to decay and brought into the glorious freedom of the children of God. (Romans 8:20–21)

In other words, God introduces futility so that we will groan and reach out to Him for liberation and salvation. King Solomon found everything meaningless in and of itself (e.g., Ecclesiastes 1:2, 14; 2:1, 11, 15, 17, 19, 21, 23, 26)—despite having access to anything his heart desired.

That's why God calls people into the marketplace. God sends us into the marketplace to liberate people from "the groan"! We are not only an occupation force; we are liberators.

How It Looks in Practice

Pastors can do certain things to alleviate the groan that men in the marketplace simply cannot do. Conversely, men in the marketplace can accomplish certain things that pastors and ministers cannot.

For example, Doug Sherman writes about a friend who owns a pallet company. Pallets are purely functional pieces used to stack goods in warehouses for trucks to transport to a new location. So the big question is, what is the eternal purpose attached to making pallets? How could a guy who manufactures pallets possibly think his work is a "calling"? How is he helping to relieve the groan?

In his book *Your Work Matters to God*, Sherman explains. Trucks filled with pallets haul Ruby Red grapefruit from the Rio Grande valley. The truck drivers pick up pallets full of cereals from Battle Creek, Michigan, and milk from Koppel, Texas, and deliver those goods to a supermarket. There, Mrs. Sherman purchases those items to make breakfast for the family. He then points out how this activity reflects the character of a God who wants to meet His children's needs.[1]

Think about all that's involved in putting breakfast on the table—all the workers with their special tasks and God-given skills. First, you have the farmers who raise the cows, grow the wheat, and tend the citrus trees. Then you have the scientists, who ensure the purity of these different foods. And you have the farm laborers and those truck drivers; then add the people who manufacture trucks and farm equipment, the people who build and maintain the highway system, and the truck-stop workers who feed the drivers. Finally, the product arrives, and the stock clerks at the grocery store bring the food items to the shelves, the cashiers ring up the sale, and the baggers place the groceries in containers and the cart.

All of those people work together to meet the needs of the Sherman family. And, of course, Mrs. Sherman herself will prepare the food for the breakfast table.

"And by the way, where are my friend's pallets in all of this?" Sherman asks. "Well, they're underneath the boxes of citrus; underneath the cereal boxes; and underneath the dairy products. So, my friend is integrally involved in making my world a better place."[2]

Why does God call men to markets? In response to the tremendous groaning brought on by the fall. God wants to take care of His children. In fact, because of His common grace, He wants to take care of everybody!

So the pallet builder is a liberator. And so are you. Whether you make pallets or hang drywall, God will use your work to fulfill His purposes. No matter what you're doing, God can use you in your employment, because you are part of a system that is liberating people from the groan.

Obviously we're not talking about salvation here. We're not discussing eternal implications yet. We are talking about the temporal, because God loves the world He made. He put us here, and His intention is that we will take care of it and it will take care of us.

Chameleons: We Adapt to the Culture

It would be great if we could live our lives inside a Christian world where Christ ruled with complete justice, where everyone was completely honest, where the best ideas always prevailed, where human effort was fairly compensated, and where everyone always wanted the best for you and you for them.

Paul the Chameleon

Instead, Christianity is lived inside cultures. Let me explain the biblical concept, then how it applies to your work life. The apostle Paul didn't try to "change" culture. Instead, he was more than willing to accommodate—make that *engage* —the culture.

> To the Jews I became like a Jew, to win the Jews. To those under the law I became like one under the law (though I myself am not under the law), so as to win those under the law. To those not having the law I became like one not having the law (though I am not free from God's law but am under Christ's law), so as to win those not having the law. To the weak I became weak, to win the weak. I have become all things to all men so that by all possible means I might save some. (1 Corinthians 9:20–22)

Why was Paul such a chameleon? Because he understood that Christianity is lived inside cultures. Christianity is not a culture of its own. That's why Paul didn't fret over customs and traditions. That's why Paul didn't give a second thought to . . .

- circumcising Timothy while preaching elsewhere that it wasn't necessary (Acts 16:3).
- telling Philemon to take back his slave, Onesimus, as a brother without calling for the abolition of slavery (Philemon 10, 17).
- shaving his head and paying to purify himself and four others in accordance with Jewish law while elsewhere saying we are no longer under the law (Acts 21:23–24).

Of course, Paul was a tiger when it came to doctrine. We never change the message, but we should always deliver the message in the way a particular culture is most likely to respond—whether Asians, the Generation Y, gays, bikers, or executives. Francis Schaeffer put it this way: "Each generation of the church in each setting has the responsibility of communicating the gospel in understandable terms, considering the language and thought-forms of that setting." It is our duty.

By calling men to Christ we are not calling them to an ancient culture. In fact, we're not calling them to any specific culture at all. Instead, we are calling them to the living Christ. Jesus is alive, and He lives inside cultures. If we want to be where He is, we must live our Christianity inside cultures too. Let's explore a few ways this might be applied to a life of work.

"In" but Not "Of," yet "Into"

Many people are convinced they are going to heaven but are content to let the world go to hell. Jesus said we are "in" but not "of" the world, but He didn't stop there. He also said, "As you sent me into the world, I have sent them into the world" (John 17:18).

If Christianity is lived inside cultures, then what is our responsibility to our business and work culture? Jesus wants to send us to improve our culture. I have already shown you how we are an occupation force and liberators. We are also ambassadors who bring the civilization of the gospel. Christians stabilize culture.

> *OUR ASSIGNMENT IS TO REPRESENT GOD WITHIN THE WORK CULTURE.*

Consider Joseph in Egypt, Daniel in Babylon, and Mordecai in Persia—three true believers who rose to high positions in non-Christian cultures. They were ambassadors for God—and stabilizing influences—inside their cultures.

It is not our assignment to create a Christian business culture. Our assignment is to represent God within the work culture—to bring salt and light into the workplace. To do that, we have to go "into" the culture. On matters not specifically commanded or prohibited by Scripture, we adapt to the culture. We don't require the culture to adapt to us. That's how Paul did it.

Paul was such a chameleon. He knew that by becoming all things to all men, he might save some (see 1 Corinthians 9:22). That's why you and I should be chameleons too.

No religion has worked as effectively as Christianity to free people from "the groan." God calls men to markets in order to make the world a better place. He seeks disciples who will effectively introduce his principles into a secular environment, for the purpose of relieving human suffering and improving the well-being of mankind.

Investors and Risk-Takers: Increasing Your Yield

One thing that Scripture makes quite clear is that God created us to do good works—to produce a crop. In the parable of the talents discussed earlier, producing a return was linked to taking risks.

Tony Campolo's book *Who Switched the Price Tags?* recorded the results of a sociology study involving fifty people, age ninety-five and older. Researchers asked these participants one question: "If you could live your life over again, what would you do differently?" Three answers dominated the results:

"I would reflect more."

"I would risk more."

"I would do more things that would live on after I am dead."

How can you increase your impact? Take more risks! God takes pleasure in our willingness to assume risk to grow His influence in the world.

A PRAYER YOU CAN PRAY

Lord Jesus, it is so challenging to come to grips with the reality of Your Word, which tells me that making a pallet to go under a crate of Ruby Red grapefruit is just as important as leading a Bible study or sharing my faith with another man. Lord, the whole creation is groaning, and those of us whom You have called to the marketplace—we are the liberators. You have put us in charge until You get back.

We pray that we might be found faithful. In Jesus' name, amen.

Questions for Personal Reflection or Group Discussion

1. What is the main thing that God is always doing?

2. We have been put in charge until Christ returns. Give an example of how you might take charge through your work.

3. What does the Bible say about the purposes of our work in Ephesians 2:10; John 15:8; Colossians 3:17, 22–24; and 1 Thessalonians 4:11–12?

4. What are God's purposes for you *personally* as a man of God in the markets of men? Knowing this, what is one thing you can do today that will increase your impact?

CHAPTER

3

INTEGRITY:

The **TEN** Commandments and the **GOLDEN RULE**

ONCE WHEN THE OFFICE RENTAL MARKET was at its lowest point here in Orlando, tenants were being offered eighteen months' free rent on a five-year lease. A woman who worked for us was promoted to leasing agent. After a long drought, she found a tenant who wanted about five thousand square feet.

Unfortunately, it was a man with one of the worst reputations in town. To make matters worse, the lease was drawn to a corporation with no personal guarantees. I rejected the offer, but this being her first deal and being quite hungry, she pleaded her case.

Against my better judgment, I told her, "If you can get a personal guarantee, we can do the lease." After several days of wrangling, she returned to say that he wouldn't sign personally—only the corporation. She was desperate to make the deal work, the building wasn't renting anyway, and for reasons I'll never understand, I eventually okayed the deal. My bad.

One Monday morning eighteen months later, I learned that five thousand square feet of space we had was empty. The "corporation" we had leased to was gutted, with no real assets. Not that I was surprised. The clever man had found a way to be in business rent free for a year and a half. The lost rent amounted to about $350,000, but that was that.

One evening a year later, I took my son to an Orlando Magic basketball game. I was able to score some excellent seats in about the twentieth row. Every time the Magic did something good, the guy who wouldn't pay his rent—down in the courtside seats—leaped to his feet in exuberant pleasure. Why not? I was paying for his tickets.

A few years later I heard that he had died suddenly. I recalled Jesus' penetrating question, "For what does it profit a man to gain the whole world, and forfeit his soul?" (Mark 8:36 NASB).

The single most important attribute in business is integrity. Integrity—and its offspring, trust—are the linchpins that hold business together. All that's needed to highlight its importance is to watch the chaos created when integrity is absent or compromised. One weasel can a lot of damage do.

Anyone with a lengthy history in business and a good reputation earned that reputation by having integrity, regardless of whether he is a Christian. Sometimes it appears as if the weasels are getting away with their greed and fraud, but eventually they all get caught. "Your sins will find you out," the Bible says.

But it's even more important for Christians to have integrity, because, like it or not, our actions reflect positively or negatively on our God. So any discussion of what it means to be a Christian at work must delve into integrity.

The Biblical Case for Integrity

We know that integrity is important to God, because the Bible says so much about it. Consider the great men of the Bible—Abraham, Joseph, Moses, Joshua, Job, David, Daniel, Mordecai, Nehemiah, Paul, and, of course, Jesus. Their careers, and failures, were always linked to their integrity.

Think about the integrity of Joseph, who was tempted to commit adultery with his boss's wife, but resisted. Or the integrity of Job, described in Scripture as "the finest man in all the earth. He is blameless—a man of complete integrity. He fears God and stays away from evil" (Job 1:8 NLT). Yet when his business empire was routed, he gave God glory and said, "Naked I came from my mother's womb, and naked I shall return. . . . Blessed be the name of the Lord" (1:21 NASB).

What if you have, or have already had, a moral failure? That's certainly not the end of you. David, who was also quite a businessman, held on to his integrity, except in the case of Uriah and Bathsheba. He even tried to conceal his sin. But once confronted, he threw himself on the mercy of God in genuine repentance, and God forgave him.

Knowing he was forgiven, he boldly asked God to judge him according to his integrity (Psalm 7:8), and in the face of danger from his enemies, he also noted, "May integrity and uprightness protect me" (Psalm 25:21). Later the Bible refers to David as someone who shepherded his people "with integrity of heart" (Psalm 78:72). David made a comeback, and so can you.

A Son of Proverbs

As you might expect, the wisdom recorded in the book of Proverbs puts a huge emphasis on integrity. "The man of integrity walks securely" (Proverbs 10:9). "The integrity of the upright guides them" (Proverbs 11:3).

Early in my business career, someone suggested that I read a chapter of Proverbs every day. Since there are 31 chapters in Proverbs, that meant I reread the book each month.

After several years of doing this, I found "proverbs" popping into my head whenever I encountered a situation that required wisdom or courage (or both). For example, when tempted to talk too much, I remembered Proverbs 10:19: "When words are many, sin is not absent, but he who holds his tongue is wise." Another time, getting angry, I recalled Proverbs 15:1: "A gentle answer turns away wrath, but a harsh word stirs up anger." Once, falsely accused, I recalled the proverb, "Like a fluttering sparrow or a darting swallow, an undeserved curse does not come to rest" (26:2).

Also, I started quoting proverbs to my friends when they seemed to be grasping for advice and direction. I would say something like, "Well, I don't know what you should do, but you'll never guess what I was reading in the book of Proverbs today!" And then I'd tell them. They seemed to be genuinely helped, and they told their friends.

Before long, men were dropping by my office to find out what I had been reading in Proverbs.

One day, my friend Tom Skinner said, "You have become a son of Proverbs."

I asked, "What do you mean?"

He pointed out that over twenty verses in Proverbs start with the words, "My son . . ."

One very practical way to strengthen your resolve to be a man of integrity is to become "a son of Proverbs."

The Standard for Integrity

The apostle Paul gave Titus, one of his mentees, this advice to pass on to the young men Titus was mentoring: "In everything set them an example by doing what is good. In your teaching show integrity, seriousness and soundness of speech that cannot be condemned, so that those who oppose you may be ashamed because they have nothing bad to say about us" (Titus 2:7–8).

The Gold Standard: The Ten Commandments and the Golden Rule

What are the specifics for integrity? Is there a "code" or "standard" to which you should hold yourself accountable? Actually, there is: the Ten Commandments and the Golden Rule. The Bible records the Ten Commandments twice, in Exodus 20 and Deuteronomy 5. They are God's very specific instructions for our conduct, and the last four, in particular, apply to our business practices and how we treat people:

- You shall not commit adultery.
- You shall not steal.
- You shall not give false testimony against your neighbor.
- You shall not covet your neighbor's house. You shall not covet your neighbor's wife, or his manservant or maidservant, his ox or donkey, or anything that belongs to your neighbor.

The Golden Rule in Matthew 7:12 says, "So in everything, do to others what you would have them do to you, for this sums up the Law and the Prophets."

In January 1984, President Ronald Reagan spoke to the National Religious Broadcasters Association in Washington, D.C. Here's a portion of his speech:

> Government bureaucracies spend billions for problems related to drugs, alcoholism and disease. How much of that money could we save, how much better off might Americans be if all of us tried a little harder to live by the Ten Commandments and the Golden Rule? I've been told that since the beginning of civilization millions and millions of laws have been written. I've even heard someone suggest it was as many as several billion. And yet, taken all together, all those millions and millions of laws have not improved on the Ten Commandments one bit.[1]

In a lot of ways, President Reagan was right. It really is as simple as studying and believing the Ten Commandments and the Golden Rule so that they become the internal standard by which we act and react to everyday situations. God's standard for integrity is found in the Ten Commandments and the Golden Rule. You don't have to look further.

PepsiCo: "It's Good for Business, and It's the Right Thing to Do"

When Steve Reinemund was CEO of PepsiCo—the parent company for the 17-billion-dollar brands of Quaker, Gatorade, Tropicana, Frito Lay, and Pepsi—he learned a valuable lesson from some business students.

Steve was invited to speak at Stanford Business School's "View From the Top," a forum for CEOs to interact with, in this case, about five hundred MBA students.

Steve spent thirty minutes outlining his diversity initiative—a hallmark of his tenure as CEO. He explained how he wanted the whole organization—from the boardroom to the front line—to look like the consumers they served because, as he told them, "A more diverse workforce is good for business."

As soon as he finished, a student popped up and asked, "I'm convinced from your presentation that it was good for business, and I'm convinced that you believe it's good for business. My question is, would you do it if it weren't good for business?"

Steve said, "I sort of stepped back and reformulated the things I said, and said it again. The same student stood up and said, 'In all due respect, you didn't answer my question.'"

Steve continued, "So I sort of fumbled around a little more, and he sat down. Then the next student stood up and said, 'Now, I have to say, in all due respect, you didn't answer his question.'

"So I went through it again—I don't know if I did any better or not—but I left there really troubled by the whole encounter because I couldn't figure out what was going on in this dynamic.

"Then one morning about two weeks later I was on a treadmill, and it came to me like a bolt of lightning. They were talking about the ethical question, but it just took me a long time to get to it. I think they felt from my presentation that I knew diversity was not only good for business but also the right thing to do, but they wanted me to come out and say it!

"I had been so programmed over my life to talk about what's good for business and to be private about the right thing to do. So now when I talk about diversity—or any other initiative—I talk about how it has to be both good for business *and* the right thing to do. We can't have one without the other.

"But it was really through that encounter with those students—they just wanted me to come out and say that diversity was not only good for business, but it was also the right thing to do. And that's exactly the kind of organizations people want to be associated with—ones that combine what's good for the business, and the right thing to do."[2]

Doing the Right Thing Even When It Hurts

Integrity also means doing the right thing even when it hurts. Skip Ast will tell you following the Golden Rule is the best choice, even if it's not the easiest choice. As president of Shasta Industries, Arizona's number one builder of pools and spas for over forty years, he faced a dilemma. His company was using a special deck coating that was guaranteed by the producer. But within two or three years, the product started peeling off the concrete where it had been used. Skip said, "We were getting an enormous number of calls on it."

Shasta Industries is the only company that gives a lifetime master insurance guarantee on its pools. But the company that produced the coating would not honor its guarantee. Skip's legal counsel said he had a great case and could recover millions of dollars. But Skip had been involved in lawsuits before, and he knew if he pursued that course of action, his customers would wait a long time for the settlement.

"So I had a decision to make," he said. "I asked myself if I really stood for the Golden Rule—do to others as you want them to do to you. Would I like to be in the place of my customer, and have the company communicate to me that there's nothing I can do with my deck right now, because the company is going through a lawsuit? Customers don't care about the lawsuits—they just want their decks fixed."

Skip decided that Shasta Industries would start its own firm to manufacture an acrylic material that would be much better than what was available before. And the company would redo all the decks with that new product. The whole process required three or four years, but Skip reported, "I retained all of my customers, and I drove home to them that we love them and will protect them, no matter what it takes. Frankly, it cost us over a million dollars, but it was the right thing to do. It was a hard decision to make, but our actions broadcast to our whole Shasta population that, when we say we stand for integrity, we put our money where our mouth is."[3]

How to Modify Your Behavior

Most observers agree we are in the middle of an integrity crisis. I personally know dishonesty is rampant among the clerks and cashiers where I get my Starbucks and movie tickets—because they often try to give me a price break as though, together, we are "sticking it to the man."

Most men face ongoing temptations to lie to get a sale, not work a full day, "borrow" supplies, fudge on expenses, not report all the income, look at pornography, and cheat—these are all temptations with a masculine bent. And, of course, recent failings at the top of the corporate world have become legendary.

However, I get nervous when I hear a message or read a book that exhorts me to *behave* my way out of a situation I have *believed* my way into. For example, if a man doesn't think that it's necessary to disclose conflicts of interest, that there's nothing wrong with "looking at the menu" when it comes to women at work, or that there's nothing wrong with little white lies—it's doubtful that a "behavior modification" scheme (such as Internet filtering software) is going to change him long-term.

> ### INTEGRITY IS A CORRELATION BETWEEN MY BIBLE, MY BELIEF, AND MY BEHAVIOR.

Belief determines *behavior*. To change behavior we need a "belief modification" plan. To say it even better, we need a "heart transformation" plan. Easily the greatest way to help a man is to help him change the core affections of his heart. Any such plan, for the Christian, necessarily starts with the Bible.

A Working Definition of Integrity

So here's a good definition of integrity for a Christian: *Integrity is a one-to-one-to-one correlation between my Bible, my belief, and my behavior.*

Let me explain. In order for my life to have integrity, there needs to be a one-to-one correlation between what I read in my *Bible* and what I *believe*. But that is not enough. There must also be a one-to-one correlation between my *belief* and my *behavior*.

People will notice when there is a disconnect between our belief and our behavior. One thing that kept my own mother from true faith for so long was watching a man she worked with read his Bible every day at lunch, but then live like the Devil all afternoon.

The Difference between Dishonesty and Poor Judgment

Have you done anything dishonest that you haven't already corrected? To answer that, you must understand the difference between *dishonesty* and *poor judgment*. For instance, I remember buying a radar detector. I had wanted one for years. I don't know why, because I don't get many tickets. I didn't even want the radar detector so I could drive faster without fear of citations. I just thought it would be a Machiavellian pleasure to know where the policeman was before he knew where I was.

So I ordered a radar detector, and when it was delivered, my wife said, "Are you out of your stupid mind? What were you thinking?" Within fifteen minutes, I realized I needed to take advantage of the thirty-day money-back guarantee.

Sometimes we do stupid things. Purchasing a radar detector was nothing more than an error in judgment. But it could have become an integrity problem if I used it the wrong way.

I don't want you to end up buried under a heap of false guilt, thinking you've committed a sin, when in reality you just did something stupid. But go ahead and test yourself. Look at the Golden Rule and the Ten Commandments. Ask yourself, "Do I lie, cheat, or steal? Do I do it regularly? Am I treating my coworkers the way I want them to treat me?"

You might answer the first question "no." But consider: Do you promise deadlines that you know you don't plan to keep? Do you do personal business on company time without permission? When someone calls, and you don't want to talk to them, do you have an assistant or a coworker say you're not in? These are integrity issues.

One day in my own company, I was walking down the hall and overheard a manager order his assistant to tell a caller that he was not in. I stopped dead in my tracks. I realized that if a visiting customer had overheard that conversation, his trust in us would collapse. Why not just have your assistant say, "He can't come to the phone right now"?

What's the big deal? We all know that "big things" are important. But the simple truth is that "little things" matter too. A little dishonesty can capsize what would otherwise have been a big career. Jesus put it this way: "Whoever can be trusted with very little can also be trusted with much, and whoever is dishonest with very little will also be dishonest with much" (Luke 16:10).

A Personal Inventory

So here are some questions to ask yourself as one who should be honest and consistent in all you do:

- Do I surf the Internet on company time when the boss is on vacation or in meetings?

- Do I make telephone calls on company time (instead of at lunch or during authorized breaks)?
- Do I mark sick time on my card when I want a day off or am out of vacation days?
- Do I report all of my income?
- Do I lie to make sales?
- Do I knock off early without permission?
- Do I fudge on expenses?
- Do I "borrow" company supplies?

If you're in management or an owner, consider these additional questions:

- Do I pay fair wages?
- Do I charge fair prices?
- Do I pay fair prices?
- If it's good for business, is it also the right thing to do?
- Does my business depend on deception? In order for me to be successful, does someone have to believe a lie?

Frankly, in the area of deception, I don't think it is biblical to do business with the attitude of "Let the Buyer Beware." We have a responsibility to treat buyers fairly.

What Should You Do When You Fail?

We can avoid a lot of heartache by simply following the Ten Commandments and the Golden Rule, but the bottom line is, sometimes we fail. How should you respond when that happens? Here are several steps that lead to restoration.

1. Practice Self-Examination

Sometimes the Holy Spirit pricks my conscience about something I've done or something I'm thinking about doing. When that happens, I go to two biblical texts:

Search me, O God, and know my heart; test me and know my anxious thoughts. See if there is any offensive way in me, and lead me in the way everlasting. (Psalm 139:23–24)

Who can discern his errors? Forgive my hidden faults. Keep your servant also from willful sins; may they not rule over me. Then will I be blameless, innocent of great transgression. (Psalm 19:12–13)

The first passage seeks God's legitimate conviction of sin, not false guilt. And the second seeks forgiveness for both unintentional and intentional sins. When you blow it, this is a wonderful place to start.

2. Cease and Desist

Stop participating in the sin. You can't get past this. If God convicts you, and you know something is a sin, forsake it. There's a big difference between saying, "I don't want to do that again," and truly forsaking your sins in your heart.

True repentance is much more than simply being sorry you were caught, or even being sorry for what you've done. It's a commitment to change the behavior.

3. Make Restitution

In some cases, where deception has led to someone else's loss, restitution will be necessary. That must be decided on a case-by-case basis.

4. Commit to Obedience without Seeking a Reward

Why should you get rewarded for not stealing? Or for not lying? This is just doing what you're supposed to do.

There is no external reward for integrity, other than avoiding the consequences of sin. But there is an internal reward. There is satisfaction in obedience. As William Penn said, "Right is right even if everyone else thinks it is wrong. And wrong is wrong even if everyone else thinks it is right."

Obedience is the key to maintaining your restoration. And you can't do that on your own—you need the Holy Spirit. His power is available to help you with daily living, in your personal as well as your work life. Invite Him to lead you along.

A Group Can Help

Engaging other men in a small group provides checks and balances you will get no other way. By being open and honest with one another, you can hold one another accountable and find strength to resist temptation. Obviously, we have to earn trust from one another by holding things in confidence. But we all need others to hold us accountable for our attitudes and actions. I'm not talking about submitting to some kind of spiritual "boss." I'm talking about being vulnerable with some fellow pilgrims, so you can help one another to avoid a breach of integrity.

But groups are also helpful after integrity has already been breached, when we need help to walk down the road of restoration. Galatians 6:1–2 explains, "Brothers, if someone is caught in a sin, you who are spiritual should restore him gently. But watch yourself, or you also may be tempted. Carry each other's burdens, and in this way you will fulfill the law of Christ." Hard to do if you don't have "brothers."

In the movie *Seabiscuit*, horse owner Charles Howard and trainer John Smith prepare Seabiscuit for great things. But when the horse is ailing, Howard contemplates getting rid of the animal. Smith responds, "You don't throw a whole life away just because it's banged up a little bit." Later in the movie, Smith plans to fire his badly injured jockey. Now Howard gives back the trainer's own words: "You know, you don't throw a whole life away just because it's banged up a little bit."

Similarly, we don't discard a brother just because he's banged up a little bit. We don't turn our backs on each other. Because we are brothers in Christ, we work to restore each other. And then we hold each other accountable to a high standard. Together we submit to this chapter's "big idea": *God's standard for integrity is found in the Ten Commandments and the Golden Rule.*

A PRAYER YOU CAN PRAY

Lord Jesus, thank You so much for making it so crystal clear, so easy to follow, so easy to understand—Your standard is found in the Ten Commandments and the Golden Rule. Lord, help me to develop [keep] that one-to-one-to-one correlation between my Bible, my beliefs, and my behavior. Where I need restoration, help me to begin with repentance, seeking Your forgiveness and Your sustaining power for obedience.

May Your Spirit grant me wisdom for each step I need to take. I ask this in Jesus' name, amen.

Questions for Personal Reflection
or Group Discussion

1. Do you have a personal standard for your business integrity, and if so, what is it? How do you feel about adopting the Ten Commandments and the Golden Rule as your standard?

2. Was there anything in the section "A Personal Inventory" that rattled you a little (or a lot)? Why or why not?

3. This chapter made a number of suggestions about what to do when we fail in our integrity. Do you need to act on any of those suggestions, and if so, what do you plan to do?

CHAPTER

4

PERFORMANCE:

What Is Our **DUTY** on the **JOB?**

JOB PERFORMANCE CAN PUT a lot of pressure on both bosses and employees, especially in a continually downsizing and transitioning economy. A consistent, quality effort is one of our key responsibilities on the job.

You have to perform—whether you're a maintenance man, line worker, or senior manager. Failure to perform at any position weakens overall effectiveness.

But the Bible also commands us to love and serve others—from the CEO to the "least of these" workers. Failure to love and serve others weakens the power of the gospel to transform lives—including those with whom we work.

Two Essentials

Performance and love. For a Christian in the workplace, both are essential. How do you balance the need to perform and produce measurable results with the command that we have to love and serve others? How do these two concepts work together in practice?

You already know that God commands us to love Him and love our neighbors. He wants us to be in right relationship with Him and right relationship with each other (see chapter 2). These are the two most important things God requires —they are His "main thing."

Our Duty to Jesus Christ

We've all heard employers talk disparagingly about specific workers. They might say something like, "Bob just isn't getting it done for the company."

And we've all heard men complain about their bosses, saying something like, "I just can't work for Vince anymore."

If we ever hope to find the balance between performance and love, we must stop focusing on Bob and Vince, and start focusing on Jesus Christ. The Bible clearly says to get our focus off the "horizontal" and onto the "vertical." As a boss or as an employee, what is our duty to Christ in the marketplace?

It's not, "What is my duty to my customer?" That's important, yes, but even more important is to focus on my duty to Jesus Christ. It is the Lord Jesus Christ whom I'm serving, not merely my customer, client, patient, investor, or boss. That's the big idea of this chapter: *Whether I'm the employee or the boss, my first duty is always to serve Jesus Christ.* We serve Jesus when we obey the commands to love God and those around us (Matthew 22:37–39; Mark 12:29–31). In this chapter, we will focus on illustrating many practical ways to balance performance and loving people.

The Bible offers guidance for "neighbor love" in the workplace—how employers and employees should treat each other, and why. Let's start with employees.

An Employee's Duty to Jesus Christ

Why do we work hard? Why do we pursue excellence? Obviously we all do our jobs for the "horizontal" reasons—rewards like a bigger paycheck, bigger offices, and more vacation time.

But honestly, once we've worked long enough, we find those horizontal perks don't provide enough motivation for a Christian to be enthusiastic and passionate about what he's doing.

Paul writes,

> Slaves, obey your earthly masters in everything; and do it, not only when their eye is on you and to win their favor, but with sincerity of heart and reverence for the Lord. *Whatever you do, work at it with all your heart, as working for the Lord, not for men,* since you know that you will receive an inheritance from the Lord as a reward. It is the Lord Christ you are serving. (Colossians 3:22–24; italics added)

The word that best summarizes the attitude that can sustain an employee is *wholeheartedness.* To be *wholehearted* you have to be motivated to do your work for Christ. Your motivation is that you really are working for and serving our Lord Jesus Christ.

It's not about doing your duty to the customer. Certainly, that's important. But wholeheartedness comes from focusing on your duty to Jesus Christ. To be wholehearted, we must serve Jesus Christ first, and then our boss and our customers. What does "wholeheartedness" look like in practice?

Practical Suggestions for Employees

First, *wholeheartedness means to do your work with excellence and integrity.* You might have a good boss this year and a bad boss next year. But because your primary allegiance is to Jesus Christ, your motivation to do an honest day's work doesn't depend on the quality of your human boss.

Second, *wholeheartedness means making sure your boss knows what you need to be successful.* Is it more tools or better equipment? An updated computer or library? More staff? More advertising? If you don't have adequate resources to perform your job with excellence, you have a responsibility to tell your boss what you need. Don't complain to others—that's what pagans do. Tell your employer what you need to be successful.

Third, *wholeheartedness means taking the initiative to improve your performance.* Maybe there's a book you can read, or a course you can take, or a seminar you can attend. Perhaps you need training for making decisions or setting priorities or managing your time. When it comes to training, tell your boss, and maybe it will make the budget.

By increasing your skills in those areas, you are serving your employer, because you will increase your productivity. And by serving your employer, you will live up to your duty to Jesus Christ.

Here's a personal productivity idea I use that's been around for a long time. Management consultant Ivy Lee was once hired to help Charles Schwab, then president of Bethlehem Steel, with some performance and productivity issues. Lee observed that in the morning, people seemed to just stand around, not sure exactly what they were supposed to do. He gave Mr. Schwab a simple idea.

> *WHOLEHEARTEDNESS MEANS BEING CONTENT WITH WHAT YOU HAVE.*

"Have your people write down in the order of importance the top ten most important things they're supposed to do during the day," Lee said. "Then tell them to start with item number one. When they're finished, move on to the second item, and so forth, until they come to the end of the day. If they've only done six of the ten things, tell them not to worry about it, because at least they've done the six most important things."

Schwab thought this was a little elementary, so he dismissed it. But Lee challenged him to try it for thirty days. "Then," he said, "just pay me whatever you think it's worth."

A month later, Lee received a check for $25,000. That was a hefty payment, considering the average worker at that time was making about two dollars a day. Schwab said it was the most important business lesson he ever learned.[1]

Fourth, wholeheartedness means being content with what you have. After I spoke during a prayer breakfast in Great Falls, Montana, a man handed me a little sheet of paper that I still keep in the front of my Bible. It simply says, "I have enough; I am enough."

Isn't that amazing? I can't tell you how many times that has centered me. Contentment is a useful tool in our effort to reflect the image of Jesus, and it also is evidence of the changes He is making in us.

A Boss's Duty to Jesus Christ

Paul wrote, "Masters, provide your slaves with what is right and fair, because you know that you also have a Master in heaven" (Colossians 4:1). As a leader in your company, be sure to honor Christ by treating your employees in a way that is right and fair.

When Moses was eighty years old, the Lord recalled him from forty years of exile in the wilderness to rescue God's people from slavery in Egypt. That was the work he was to perform.

"Let my people go," Moses and Aaron, his brother, told the pharaoh. But the king was cruel. He said, "The Hebrew slaves have too much time on their hands" (paraphrase of Exodus 5:1, 8b). So he ordered his middle managers to stop providing the straw that the Israelites needed to make bricks. But the pharaoh didn't reduce their quota. Same quota, fewer resources. That's downsizing.

What's the problem with downsizing? When you downsize an organization, you must upsize the responsibilities of the remaining employees. In essence, they have the same quota, but not as much straw.

The "employees" were dispirited. They couldn't even "hear" words of hope from God. God sent Moses to remind the people of their coming deliverance from slavery. "But when Moses delivered this message to the Israelites, they didn't even hear him—they were that beaten down in spirit by the harsh slave conditions" (Exodus 6:9 MESSAGE).

That's what happens when you don't do your duty to Jesus Christ as a boss. When you don't do what is fair and right, you beat down your employees. And the problem is, they don't just feel beaten down at work—they feel beaten down everywhere.

I'm sure that at some point, you've experienced harsh treatment from an unfair boss. And it closed up your spirit—so dispirited you that you couldn't even hear good news!

As a boss, you can put people under such harsh treatment that they can't even hear a word of hope from God Himself. So if you are a Christian boss, your duty to Jesus Christ is to treat people with fairness and justice. It's not about doing your duty to "Bob." It's about doing your duty to Jesus Christ.

Practical Suggestions for Employers

What does "fair and right" look like in practice? First, *fair and right means that you provide decent wages, normal working hours, clear expectations, appreciation, and honest feedback*. These are the basics. Without these factors in place it is doubtful anyone is going to say, "I really have a good boss."

Second, *fair and right means having the courage to resolve conflicts*. Most people don't. Instead, they build up little grudges against everyone around them. They have a "knock" on everyone, because everyone has let them down. Instead, try to deal with nonperformance or relationship issues immediately and directly. For example, I like to start such conversations with, "Bill, we need to have an awkward conversation," then explain my side of the story, then ask for his.

Third, *fair and right means resisting the temptation to form "triangles" against anyone*. A triangle is two people ganging up on a third person—often behind the person's back.

Fourth, *fair and right means honestly assessing performance*. This is best done "as you go" rather than by shocking an employee at an annual performance review. Nothing said at an annual review should come as a surprise. Likewise, fair and right means not glossing over areas that need improvement because they make you feel uncomfortable. Personally, I have found Ken Blanchard's "One Minute Reprimands" from *The One Minute Manager* a useful technique.

Fifth, *fair and right means creating an environment where employees can flourish and grow*. That could mean the physical environment, but it surely means a loving environment where people are honored and respected.

Sixth, *fair and right means not punishing people for the failings of the system*. This is an idea from W. Edwards Deming, widely credited with improving production in the United States during World War II and also for his work in Japan. Your work system is perfectly designed to produce the results you are getting. So look at fixing the system first, before blaming the people.

Seventh, *fair and right means dismantling jobs in which people consistently fail*. The late management expert Peter Drucker—a Christian, by the way—labeled some jobs as "Widow Makers." In nineteenth-century New England, every now and then, one of the fishing vessels would inexplicably have many more injuries and deaths than were expected. Rather than waste time—and lives—trying to fix the ship, they would dismantle it.

Drucker wrote that if you have a position where two or three people in a row have failed, you may have a "Widow Maker" on your hands. If you're serious about doing your duty to Jesus Christ, you may need to dismantle it.

Eighth, *fair and right means moving people out of positions not suited for them.* If Bob just can't fulfill the duties for his benefit, as well as the company's, he needs to be moved to another position. If there is no suitable position in the company, you need to let him go so he can find a place where he can celebrate his giftedness. If you leave Bob in a position that he cannot handle, because of his own ineffectiveness or the system's, nobody will feel more beaten down than Bob. And frankly, you will be his Pharaoh.

So if you have a "Bob" who's not getting it done, you have a duty to Jesus Christ either to give him adequate resources, to move him to another position, or to help him find a position in a different organization where he can be more productive.

So whether you are a boss or an employee, if you want to figure out how to balance the need to perform with the command to love and serve others, the question to ask yourself is, "What is my duty to Jesus Christ?" For the employee, it is wholeheartedness. For the employer, it is being fair and right.

A PRAYER YOU CAN PRAY

Heavenly Father, thank You for Your Word—how clear it is; how concise; how it shows us how employees and bosses should treat each other and why. Thank You, Lord, that we have something bigger than just each other by which we can be motivated, and that is our duty to Jesus Christ. In His name I now pray. Amen.

Questions for Personal Reflection
or Group Discussion

1. If you are an employee, do you feel a lot of pressure to perform? If yes, give an example. If you are a boss, do you feel a lot of pressure to perform and/or to motivate employees to perform? If yes, give an example.

2. How should employees and bosses act toward one another, according to this chapter?

3. Compare how your work environment looks with your answer to question 2. How many job performance issues in your work could be resolved by observing the ideas presented in this chapter? What can you do differently over the next several days for your boss or employees?

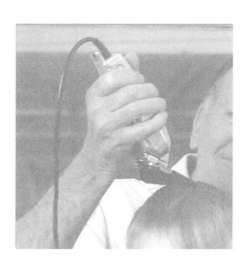

CHAPTER

PEOPLE:

NEIGHBOR-LOVE at Work

DEPENDING ON YOUR JOB, you will spend anywhere from one to six hours with people every working day—bosses, employees, peers, vendors, investors, clients, patients, customers. Our ability to handle these relationships will definitely affect our work performance, but it also will *define* our success as a Christian in the workplace.

Serving people is the purpose of work—because the sovereign God is always orchestrating all human events to bring people into right relationship with Him and right relationship with each other. For God, the relationship *is* the task.

It's a Messy Business

For whatever reasons, we live in an age of difficult people. Increasingly, these people bring a growing number of dysfunctions to work and the marketplace.

As a result, people skills are increasingly important in the workplace. But it's not easy. For example, research indicates the number one reason that CEOs fail in their positions has to do with their people skills.

People are a confluence of complexity and an amalgamation of inconsistencies. Some employees can't—or won't—perform. Some bosses pout like little dictators. Some customers can't be satisfied—others refuse to be satisfied.

It's messy, but these are the people with whom we are called to interact—and influence—for the sake of Christ's kingdom. As a friend says, "Relationships are messes worth making."

What should be different about the way that we, as Christians, interact with people at work?

The Starting Point Is Love

We should begin with love. Jesus said, "A new command I give you: Love one another. As I have loved you, so you must love one another. By this all men will know that you are my disciples, if you love one another" (John 13:34–35).

What was "new" about the new commandment? The "as I have loved you" part was new.

What did Jesus say? In essence, "People will know you are My disciples by the way you love them."

Love is the active ingredient in the "right relationship with each other" part of "the main thing" God is doing (as discussed in chapter 2). Love is the glue that holds us together, and the oil that keeps us from rubbing each other the wrong way.

Love is how we demonstrate that we are disciples of Jesus. Love is what creates interest in the gospel. Love is what gives us power when we speak. Love is our proof of discipleship. In essence, Jesus said how we treat people on the job doesn't only affect our reputation—it affects His reputation as well.

For Christian faith to be attractive to worldly people, there has to be a difference about us that recommends our faith. That difference is love.

Love Equals Service

How did Jesus love us? Jesus said, "Whoever wants to be great must be a servant, for I did not come to be served, but to serve, and to give My life as a ransom for many. Now that I have washed your feet, you should wash one another's feet. I have set an example that you should do as I have done for you" (adapted from Matthew 20:26–28; John 13:14–15).

The heart of love is service. In our work, to serve is the most practical expression of neighbor love. Love is what love does. You won't be washing anyone's feet on the job, of course, but you may offer to help a coworker meet a deadline or pour a cup of coffee for someone who reports to you. These small but practical acts of service have value in and of themselves—even if you never, ever talk about Jesus.

Difficult-to-Love People

During His Sermon on the Mount, Jesus gives practical advice on how to love difficult people. "You have heard that it was said, 'Eye for eye, and tooth for tooth.' But I tell you, Do not resist an evil person. If someone strikes you on the right cheek, turn to him the other also. And if someone wants to sue you and take your tunic, let him have your cloak as well. If someone forces you to go one mile, go with him two miles" (Matthew 5:38–41).

What does Jesus mean? Are these actual, specific actions He wants to see from His followers? I think He is making a case for an attitude of nonretaliation and tolerance. He's saying He wants us to be thermostats rather than thermometers. He wants us to measure our culture and change its "temperature," rather than simply recording it. He's saying, "I don't want you simply to adjust to other people. I want you to live in a certain way, so people can tell you're My disciples." Yes, some people are going to mistreat us, and we are to practice nonretaliation and tolerance.

Verse 43 picks up the continuation of Jesus' sermon in *The Message*, a paraphrase written by Eugene Peterson:

"You're familiar with the old written law, 'Love your friend,' and its unwritten companion, 'Hate your enemy.' I'm challenging that. I'm telling you to love your enemies. Let them bring out the best in you, not the worst. When someone gives you a hard time, respond with the energies of prayer, for then you are working out of your true selves, your God-created selves. This is what God does. He gives his best—the sun to warm and the rain to nourish—to everyone, regardless: the good and the bad, the nice and the nasty. If all you do is love the lovable, do you expect a bonus? Anybody can do that. If you simply say hello to those who greet you, do you expect a medal? Any run-of-the-mill sinner does that."

[Jesus adds,] "In a word, what I'm saying is, Grow up. You're kingdom subjects. Now live like it. Live out your God-created identity. Live generously and graciously toward others, the way God lives toward you."

Grin and Bear It?

But if we're not careful, we'll see Jesus' ethic as "grin and bear it." A lot of Christians are grinning and bearing—and then begrudging.

If you've never been taught how to express disagreement constructively and resolve conflict when you have a problem, you will stuff it—at least on the job. Real and perceived injustices, large and small, build up a volcano of grudges and anger just waiting to explode. Sometimes the wife and dog bear the brunt of it. Left unchecked, even Christians end up with funny creases on their faces, shoulders stooped in resignation, and find themselves yelling at the evening news.

Obviously, that's not the response Jesus had in mind when He told us to love our enemies. That's not what Jesus would do—He would never just grin and bear it. Scripture shows that when Jesus saw something wrong, He fixed it. He's not asking you to be a grin-and-bear-it Christian.

Instead, He's calling us to live with an attitude of grace. He wants His followers to live generously toward other people—to forgive them regardless of whether or not they seek forgiveness. So, what does that look like at a practical level in the contemporary work world?

Neighbor-Love at Work

Management expert Peter Drucker said, "The purpose of a business is to create and keep customers." What would the Jesus way of creating and keeping customers look like?

The Jesus way is to love and serve. On the upside, to love and serve means that we exceed people's expectations for how we treat them—we go the second mile.

On the flipside, however, to love and serve doesn't mean that we lower our expectations for how people treat us. In other words, to love someone doesn't mean you let them get away with mistreating you or others, not paying their bills as agreed, routinely missing deadlines, making promises they don't keep, and so on. That's not loving them; that's enabling them to continue bad behavior.

Obviously, such genuine love can be difficult, because sometimes customers can seem unlovable. Jesus asks us to love them anyway, whatever their behavior—though I don't think "cheek striking" is to be taken as literally allowing physical contact. It is spoken in the style of hyperbole (overstating the case to make the point).

I will love and serve you best not by lowering my expectations of you, but by increasing my expectations of myself.

> *I WILL LOVE AND SERVE YOU BEST . . . BY INCREASING MY EXPECTATIONS OF MYSELF.*

For instance, what do you do with a customer who commits to a deal with you, but then strings you along for six months? After a while, you can get bitter about it. You can nurse a grudge. Instead, why not just call the person and say, "Look, it has been six months. I think it would be smart for us to bring this to a conclusion, unless you see a compelling reason that hasn't yet been brought to my attention."

The customer could have lots of reasons he's embarrassed to talk about. Perhaps he is in the middle of selling something and he's getting strung along too, or he's going after financing, or maybe he's had financial reverses.

Another example is someone with whom you have a payment dispute. What does turning the other cheek look like there? Certainly it doesn't mean not collecting payment.

When I was discharged from the army, I went to work for GMAC Finance as a bill collector for a few months before college. My boss was a great mentor who told me, "Pat, you have a responsibility toward your customers. When people don't pay, it's for one of three reasons: They *can't* pay, they *won't* pay, or they *shouldn't* pay."

Before taking action against a nonpaying client, he said I should figure out which category matched the situation. "If they can't pay," he said, "we work with them. If they have money and won't pay, we work with them in a different way. And if we have a dispute on the account, and they shouldn't pay, we have to deal with that first." What a gracious way of dealing with nonpaying customers.

Self-Evaluation

At some point every person in your life is going to irritate you. You have to decide:

- Will you be a grin-and-bear-it Christian?
- Or will you have the courage to live by grace, to deal with those irritations?

If you don't choose that second option, almost without exception you will build a grudge. Right now, take a moment to examine your heart. I am certain that some readers will realize they basically have grudges against most of the people in their lives.

The big idea for this chapter is this: *For every person in your life, you can be a man of grace or a man of "grudge," but you will not be both.*

In your dealings with every customer, employee, vendor, or whomever, you will either grace them or grudge them. And frankly, when you carry a grudge, you are burning a lot of emotional energy. That's not what Jesus meant when He said, "Turn the other cheek."

How Should We Treat Employees?

Peter Drucker said that only about one-third of hiring decisions turn out to be excellent. One-third of the hires will be average, and the other one-third will be outright failures—and that's the track record for those who make the best hiring decisions.[1]

That's sobering. If you're a manager, decide up front how you will deal with employees who don't achieve your expectations. Will you grind your teeth in grin-and-bear-it incompetence? Or will you courageously confront, in love and in truth, dealing with these issues as Jesus would? And if a coworker disappoints you by not doing his fair share on a team project, will you address the issue, in love, or just pretend it didn't happen and grind your teeth in frustration?

Mentor the Weak

A friend of mine, fifteen years my junior, was having a terrible problem and was ready to fire an employee because he just wasn't getting it done. "Could I ask your advice?"

"Sure," I said. "What's up?"

"I recently hired a young man fresh out of college, and he has a terrible work ethic. At least once a week he comes to work late, several times during the day he calls his wife or his wife calls him. He goes home for lunch and, most days, comes back late. He is driving me nuts!"

What would neighbor-love do? In this case, to love and serve means to offer guidance as well as correction.

"First," I asked, "does he have a written job description? In other words, does he know what your 'ten commandments' are? You cannot punish him—it's not fair—if he doesn't understand what the expectations are." He did not have a job description, and my friend starting taking notes.

"Second," I continued, "have you published your daily expectations? Do you have a written policy manual—you know, with starting time, lunch breaks, stopping times, policies for personal business on company time, and so on? It's not fair to judge someone by a set of expectations that only you are aware of." My friend nodded and made more notes.

"Third, does this young man understand how you like to receive reports? Some people like to have written reports on a regular basis. I like to have regular written reports. I am a systematizer. Other people like to have verbal reports; they don't need it in writing. And some like them often, while others don't care as much."

So if you're dealing with a nonperforming employee, particularly on issues related to work ethic, I suggest that you begin by asking three questions:

- Has this employee received a written job description?
- Have you published some sort of general, written policy that outlines requirements for practical work issues like starting time, lunch breaks, stopping times, making or receiving personal phone calls, etc.?
- Does this person understand how you like to receive reports?

If you answer no to any of those questions, it's entirely possible that correcting those issues will improve your employee's performance.

Similarly, if you work for a manager who hasn't offered a written job description or doesn't ask for reports, and you feel confused or perhaps misunderstood by your boss, it's okay to initiate. Your involvement can clarify the situation and may impress your supervisor with your desire to do your best. A friend of mine learned that one worker was about to be fired by his entrepreneur-boss. So my friend asked the employee, "What's your reporting structure for communicating with your boss?"

The employee said, "I don't have one."

"Why don't you start giving your boss a weekly written report of what you accomplished in the last week?" That simple strategy changed everything. After two months, the boss thought that employee was terrific. So if you feel confused or misunderstood, offer your superior a report of weekly or monthly activity, or ask for a list of duties to clarify your job responsibilities.

As a manager, look for practical ways to love and serve employees. Rather than treat employees like pieces of meat or machines, tutor them. We should respond as men of grace, not as men of grudge. Instead of getting angry, and letting that build till we possibly explode and fire them, we grace them.

Recognize the Strong

And then you have employees who meet and even exceed expectations. Let's not forget them.

At Man in the Mirror, our ministry, we had a fantastic warehouseman. He used to supervise 120 people in the corporate world. Then he worked for us, and he ran a crackerjack warehouse. I don't recall ever hearing of any major problems in his area.

One day I decided to go to the warehouse. When I saw him, I said, "You know, I never hear about anything that goes wrong in here. Everything seems to run smoothly. I'm afraid I've been taking that for granted, and I wanted to tell you I really appreciate the excellent job you've been doing."

It may have been my imagination, but I think I saw tears in his eyes. He really appreciated the fact that I would take time to encourage him. I give the Holy Spirit credit for that inspiration.

Whenever you're dealing with employees, regardless of their level of performance, you should be a man of grace. That will be expressed differently in different situations. But remember—you cannot be gracious and hold a grudge at the same time.

Look for Ways to Encourage Employees—and Employers Too

We can be creative as we seek to grace our workers. For that matter, as workers, we can look for ways to encourage our employers. I once had an employer who just rubbed me the wrong way. Eventually I discovered he had a hero. While traveling in England, I stumbled on a rare yet inexpensive print of his hero, so I bought it and gave it to him as a gift.

When he opened the gift, he told me, "I really appreciate this so much. I never had a father. This man has been my father figure. Even though he's dead, I've always looked to him for guidance in my life."

I learned a lot from that experience. As I graced that man instead of continuing to grudge him, our relationship changed. He has long since stopped being my employer, but we have remained friends.

Think "Team"

If I asked you, "Are you and your wife on the same team, or are you on two competing teams?" you would instantly know the answer. She would too. It should be the same with every relationship, including those with whom you work. We should be teammates, not rivals.

As a practical application, write out a list of all your work relationships and write "Yes" or "No" next to each name, depending on whether or not you feel like you're on the same team.

If you aren't getting along with anyone in a key relationship, I recommend a book called *Crucial Conversations: Tools for Talking When Stakes Are High*, by Kerry Patterson, Joseph Grenny, Ron McMillan, and Al Switzler. A lot of men hold grudges because they don't know a practical, hands-on way to be gracious in difficult situations. This book will walk you through the issues.

The bottom line for all of this is simple. As Christians who participate in the workplace, we need to figure out how our faith will be expressed in the way we treat customers, employees, and bosses. How will we do things differently because we follow Jesus?

A PRAYER YOU CAN PRAY

Lord Jesus, thank You for Your Word. God, I am a little surprised that there can be so many misunderstandings about what You are trying to get across. Certainly this grin-and-bear-it concept is one of them. I pray You would give me victory in this area. Help me realize where I've been grudging, and where I need to develop more grace. Help me to do the practical things—to have the courage to be a man of truth, love, and service. I ask this in Jesus' name, amen.

Questions for Personal Reflection
or Group Discussion

1. If someone was watching you with an employee, boss, or customer, should they expect to see anything different, and if so, what?

2. What is the gist of John 13:34–35 and Matthew 5:38–41, 46–48 as these passages relate to work relationships? Does this mean being a doormat?

3. Our texts today indicate love as the foundation for healthy relationships. What good can love do when you have:
   - an overdemanding boss?
   - a nonperforming employee?
   - an ungrateful customer?

6

WITNESSING:

AUTHENTIC Ways
to Share Your FAITH

IF YOU ARE A CHRISTIAN IN THE WORKPLACE, you no doubt experience both the desire to witness about your faith and the tension in not knowing what to do. There are several legitimate questions you may ask:

- Is it appropriate to witness at work?
- Is it legal?
- How far can you go?
- Shouldn't people find Christ outside of work?
- Is there really a need?

Let's begin with the final question. What do men typically need? Actually, men don't "need" Christ in the same way they need gasoline when their gauge is near "empty." They don't need Jesus in the same way they need a haircut, a paycheck, or coins to cover their highway tolls. I think it's a mistake to approach nonbelievers with the assumption that they *need* Christ. When we talk to them from that viewpoint, we get frustrated because they don't "get it." The bottom line is, people want what they want—and they already have a pretty good number of things on that list. Most non-Christians don't sense an immediate need for Jesus.

Of course, at a different level, everyone does need an eternal, all-sufficient Savior. But if a man doesn't *feel* that need, you'll find it very difficult to convince him.

That doesn't mean we should give up. It simply means we should be alert to the times in people's lives when they *do* feel the need. That happens when they are in crisis. That could be a divorce, the death of a loved one, consequences of infidelity, a wayward child, an empty nest, aging parents, midlife malaise, personal health issues, or loss of purpose—to mention some of the obvious ones. During a down economy, it could mean the loss of a job, bankruptcy, or emotional depression.

Whatever the crisis, the greatest possibility in witnessing comes when a colleague faces one of these turning points. On a daily basis, we all encounter people with tremendous needs. And as Christians, we have the resources to help. Yet most of us hesitate, because we're confused or afraid or both. We really don't know our biblical responsibilities or our legal limits.

Clearing Up the Confusion

Our Mandate

What is our biblical responsibility? Christians have a mandate to be witnesses. Jesus said, "Whoever acknowledges me before men, I will also acknowledge him before my Father in heaven" (Matthew 10:32). This is the reward part of the mandate. But He then added, "But whoever disowns me before men, I will disown him before my Father in heaven." And that's the negative motivation.

Christians are to witness *everywhere* and will receive power to do so. Many Christians know Acts 1:8 from memory. This verse records the last or near-last words of Jesus. He said, "You will receive power when the Holy Spirit comes on you; and you will be my witnesses in Jerusalem, and in all Judea and Samaria, and to the ends of the earth."

True believers do feel a sense of obligation, duty, and desire to witness. We want to be counted among the faithful followers of Jesus. That faithfulness extends to the workplace just as it does to the other areas of our lives. Most of us want to witness—but we aren't sure we know how, and we don't know if we're allowed to do so.

A few years ago, Tony Blair, then prime minister of Great Britain, was questioned about his passionate support for America. He responded, "I have learned over the years, it's a pretty good test of a country to find out who wants to get in and who wants to get out. People want to get into the U.S."

Our Rights

He's absolutely right. Of course, a lot of that desire is fueled by economic opportunity. But a lot of it also is fueled by our liberties, including our freedoms of speech and religion. In the United States, our Bill of Rights clearly protects our freedom in matters of religion and expression. That's a tremendous gift and privilege not extended to people who live in many other parts of the world. Nothing legally prohibits you from being a witness for your faith in the workplace.

Within that context, though, we do need to know how to be effective in our witness. This chapter will explain how to witness *through* our work, and how to witness *at* our work.

The Demeanor of Witnessing at Work

Paul admonished the Corinthian believers: "Whether you eat or drink or whatever you do, do it all for the glory of God. Do not cause anyone to stumble, whether Jews, Greeks or the church of God—even as I try to please everybody in every way. For I am not seeking my own good but the good of many, so that they may be saved" (1 Corinthians 10:31–33).

That's a broad requirement, so let's break it down. Paul admonished believers to:

- Do everything (including your work) for God's glory.
- Avoid offending others, so you don't cause them to "stumble."
- Try to please everyone.

- Don't seek your own good, but the good of many.
- Remember that your goal is the salvation of many people.

Paul wasn't suggesting that we should be "people pleasers" at the expense of doing what God wants. On the other hand, he didn't want to intentionally put someone off with the way he lived. Our lives say more about us than our lips.

In discussing the best way to witness, a ranking executive at the Walt Disney Company once said, "Be intentional about sharing your faith and showing a real interest in the lives of those around you." This speaks to how Christians are motivated differently than non-Christians. Most nonbelievers are stuck in the rut of seeing other people as a means to achieving their goals. Christians see people differently—not just as stepping-stones on the pathway to profit, but as individuals created in God's image, and thus deserving consideration and respect.

The workplace—or anywhere else, for that matter—is no place for a "bull in a china shop." There's no place for aggressively cornering people and wearing them down with your attention. It's counterproductive—though I suspect we've all done that at some point in our Christian lives. I know I have. I remember an acquaintance named Jack who came to the Bible study that I teach. He was an attorney, and I walked with him through a crisis period—a divorce. Eventually I badgered him into saying a prayer to receive Christ. He prayed the prayer, and as soon as he could, he said good-bye and left. I've never seen him since.

Do you have the legal right to badger people? No, you have the legal right to express your religion, but not to badger anyone. As a matter of policy, in most companies you can't badger anyway. And you have an obligation to Christ not to badger. But you can witness. So let's look at some positive ways to express our faith within the context of the workplace.

The Way of Witnessing at Work

Express Faith at Work through Actions

Francis of Assisi once said, "Preach the Gospel at all times, and when necessary use words." He understood that actions speak louder than words. It's just as true in the work world as it is everywhere else.

The most excellent and most dependable workers are the best witnesses. Why? Because they show how the values of God's kingdom intersect with the values of the business world. Scripture shows a God who esteems hard work and commends the pursuit of excellence. The business world values those same characteristics. So a Christian worker who demonstrates those values will create a point of contact, because unbelieving people in his work environment respect hard work, excellence, and dependability.

As Christian philosopher Francis Schaeffer explained, "If you do your work well, you will have a chance to speak." And steel magnate An-

HAVE LOUD ACTIONS AND A QUIET VOICE.

drew Carnegie once said, "The older I get, the less I listen to what people say. I just watch what they do." *Your starting place in workplace witnessing is to do your work well for the glory of God.*

Have loud actions and a quiet voice. That's the big idea for this chapter. The daughter of a friend has mastered loud actions, quiet voice. Sometimes people respond badly to her Christian lifestyle choices. Sometimes they say, "You think you're better than I am, don't you?" But then, when they get into trouble, they say, "There's something different about you, and I want to know what it is." She chooses to live in a way that demonstrates her relationship with the Lord. She understands the value of loud actions accompanied by a quiet voice.

That's the way to express faith at work. We do our work for the glory of Christ. And we let our actions invite curiosity at times when people are ready.

Express Faith at Work through Words

Sometimes loud actions open doors for verbal testimonies. That's when we also need to understand the principles described in 1 Peter 3:15, which says, "But in your hearts set apart Christ as Lord. Always be prepared to give an answer to everyone who asks you to give the reason for the hope that you have. But do this with gentleness and respect."

That goes along with our big idea—loud actions, quiet words. One weekend I was at the Sebring International Raceway, one of the world's classic sports car race tracks. Sports car racing is one of my passions, and I was challenging Sebring in a rented race car.

I was a customer, just "being myself" at the Sebring, Florida, race track, but my behavior stood in stark contrast to some of the other racing customers. That sparked curiosity in a group of three young men, all in their twenties and thirties, who were working on our cars.

As we talked, I started telling them about my family. It quickly became clear that at least two of those young men had no positive father figures. I told a couple of stories about father things, including one that came from my friend C. R. Smith. He said that one day he came across an eight-year-old boy who was pouting and disgruntled.

"What's the matter?" he asked.

"Aw, nuthin'," the boy replied.

"Oh, come on," C. R. coaxed. "You can tell me."

"Well," the boy replied. "It's my dad."

"What about your dad?" C. R. asked.

"I don't have one," he said. "You can't do nuthin' without a dad."

As I repeated that line—"You can't do nuthin' without a dad"—tears suddenly puddled in the eyes of one young man. That opened the door for a conversation. Then another one said, "My parents divorced when I was five years old. I have a relationship with my dad, but he never taught me anything."

I was able to talk to them briefly about spiritual things, and give them each a copy of a book that talks about practical living and how to start a relationship with Christ.

And that's how witnessing works. That was the point for beginning a relationship. By my actions, I gained the right to speak. Then I initiated a conversation that uncovered the crisis point. Without offending, I talked in terms of their needs. And in relationship, I give the reason for my hope, and I purpose to do it with gentleness and respect, just as the Scriptures suggest.

Chick-fil-A: Low-Key yet Powerful

Truett Cathy, a superstar role model for Christians in business, certainly understands the value of loud actions and a quiet voice. Cathy, founder of Chick-fil-A, erects a sign in each restaurant that simply states, "Since 1946, it has been our nationwide policy to be closed on Sunday. Thank you for your patronage, and we look forward to serving you Monday through Saturday."

Probably you knew that Chick-fil-A is closed on Sundays, but perhaps you didn't know why. His son, Dan Cathy, president of Chick-fil-A, explained, "My dad grew up in a boardinghouse, and he had to wash dirty dishes on Sunday afternoon for business people who would come through and stay in their home. Dad often lamented this—a young teenager having to wash dishes when all of his buddies were out playing ball and having a good time.

"He said even back then that if he ever opened up a restaurant, he would be closed on Sunday because he didn't like to ask other people to do what he was unwilling to do himself."[1]

In 1946, Cathy opened his first restaurant, the Dwarf Grill, and, true to his promise, it was closed on Sunday—a policy the company has maintained ever since. When the Cathy family first began to open Chick-fil-A restaurants in shopping malls, being closed on Sunday wasn't an issue because the malls weren't open either.

By the time the culture shift took place and extended hours and Sunday openings became the mall norm, all their leases were already in place. And they had the option to stay closed on Sundays.

Today, the malls still go along with them closing on Sundays, but as Dan Cathy said, "We learned shopping malls could care less about our corporate purpose, but they really like the fact that we paid our rent based on a percentage of our sales. We actually report all of our sales—it's kind of tempting as a retailer not to report your entire sales—but from an ethical standpoint, they appreciate the consistency that we actually would report all of our sales."

Cathy continued, "They like the rent checks that we write, because we write them for more rent, even though we're closed on Sunday, than any other tenant could pay by being open seven days. So it was strictly a bottom-line financial decision from the developer's standpoint to give us space in a shopping mall, because they knew the demand for the product was that strong."[2]

You don't want to miss this point: God honors Chick-fil-A for keeping the Sabbath by letting them earn more revenue in six days than similar restaurants earn in seven days. Also, what a powerful witness to the authenticity of their faith that it reports all income, which of course means it must pay more rent. And what a blessing to the employees who have a day of rest.

Cathy added, "From a practical standpoint, I believe our food tastes better on Monday because we're closed on Sunday. When you've had a chance to rest and be with your family, to worship if you so choose, you're just more refreshed on Monday—our smiles are bigger."[3]

Because of its closed-on-Sunday policy, Chick-fil-A may be the highest-profile business witness in the United States. Loud actions, quiet voice. In our profit-driven world, this action speaks through a megaphone. It elevates curiosity and opens the door for a verbal response, which is quietly—and clearly—accessible from its website, which says its corporate purpose is "to glorify God by being a faithful steward of all that is entrusted to us" and "to have a positive influence on all who come into contact with Chick-fil-A."

Limitations and Opportunities

Witnessing is not about getting people to do something they don't want to do. We've already talked about not badgering people into submission. Let's look at some of the other behaviors we should avoid:

- Don't proselytize. Witnessing is sharing about your faith. Evangelism is taking someone as far as they want to go toward Jesus. Proselytizing, however, has the negative connotation of badgering someone to convert to your faith.
- Don't use your employer's time. While you're "on the clock," do your work. Otherwise, you're demonstrating a lack of integrity that will impede rather than support your witness.
- Don't discriminate against people who are not Christian.
- Avoid any appearance of doing evil.

At the same time, don't shy away when God opens an opportunity. And remember: loud actions, quiet words. My friend Scott is a perfect example of this. He used to manage a music store for a nationwide chain. A lot of his employees were in their twenties.

Scott, himself in his early thirties, explained, "I never really said anything about my beliefs, but when a customer would get steamed, I would try to treat that customer the way I thought Jesus would do it." His young employees noticed.

They'd say, "Wow! That was amazing how you handled that." They noticed his attitude and his actions, which were in alignment with God's intent. That opened the door for him to initiate relationship, which eventually gave opportunity for Scott to share his faith.

Let me assure you—this stuff is very practical. It works.

So I challenge you: Let your actions communicate your commitment to God. Then watch for the opportunity to speak your witness.[4] Perhaps it will be as simple as telling a customer, "God bless you!" Or perhaps you can invite a work acquaintance to a Bible study or to an event at your church. Perhaps you can offer to pray about a specific crisis in the person's life. Just be alert—and "be prepared to give an answer to everyone who asks you to give the reason for the hope that you have. But do this with gentleness and respect" (1 Peter 3:15). Use wisdom, common sense, and grace as you respond to the scriptural mandate to be a witness everywhere you go. You don't have to push. Evangelism is simply taking someone as far as they want to go toward Jesus.

A PRAYER YOU CAN PRAY

Lord Jesus, thank You for the freedoms You have given us in America—the freedoms of religion and expression. Even though many people don't recognize their need for You yet, we know they will face crises that will make them understand their mortality and their insufficiency. I pray that You would help me in the marketplace to be loud in my actions and quiet in my voice. Help me to earn the right to influence with the integrity and credibility of my life.

Then, when I see those strategic moments when people are ready to respond to You, help me to be a faithful witness. I ask this in Jesus' name, amen.

Questions for Personal Reflection
or Group Discussion

1. Do you feel comfortable talking about your faith in the workplace? Why or why not?

2. How do the chapter's Bible references suggest we live and talk out our faith in the workplace?

3. Are there any possibilities for sharing your faith in the marketplace that you have not fully considered, and if so, what are they?

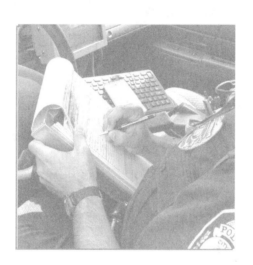

CHAPTER

7

MONEY:

PROMISES, Pleasures, and PERILS

SOME PEOPLE JUST HAVE A GIFT for making money. Scottish immigrant and steel baron Andrew Carnegie, who founded the modern corporation, was such a man.

Carnegie retired as the world's richest man at the age of sixty-six, when he sold his company in 1901 for $480 million.

He took his $225-million share of the sale proceeds and devoted the last eighteen years of his life to giving it away. For example, he funded almost three thousand public libraries throughout the United States and abroad.

But even so, Carnegie was still earning interest faster than he could give it away. By his death he had given away over $350 million and still had $30 million left!

In spite of his generosity, many religious people in his day reviled Andrew Carnegie. They demonized him for his wealth. For instance, in 1891, Rev. Hugh Price Hughes, a noted minister in England, wrote, "When I contemplate

Carnegie as the representative of a particular class of millionaires, I am forced to say with all personal respect, and without holding him in the least responsible for his unfortunate circumstances, that he is an anti-Christian phenomenon, social monstrosity, and a grave political peril."[1]

Why did Hughes and others revile Carnegie so much? They said that the world is home to vast populations of poor people, many of them living in cultures where poverty has dominated for generations. It didn't seem fair to them that so much wealth should be consolidated in one person.

Carnegie, however, was not born rich; his was the classic American rags-to-riches story. He grew up dirt-poor, but God gave him a knack for business and making money. Granted, the working conditions of his day were suspect, but the religious revilers didn't take into account that for poor people to make progress, they need jobs. Employees cannot exist without employers.

All people everywhere want to improve their lots in life. The desire to make a better life is one of our most innate, noble, and God-given characteristics. This motivation is both natural and spiritual. It is a part of the way God created us. So, of course, the Bible has a lot to say about God's perspective on money and wealth, much of which we will earn through our work.

A Biblical Perspective on Wealth

A good place to start is with Jesus' parable about the shrewd manager (Luke 16:1–9). The story goes something like this: Once upon a time a wealthy man employed a manager to oversee his holdings. The boss heard that his manager was wasting his wealth, so he confronted and fired the man.

But the story takes an unexpected turn. In response to being fired, the manager contacted all of his employer's debtors and offered to cut the amount they owed in half. Luke 16:8–9 records Jesus' surprise ending—the master ended up commending the dishonest manager because he acted shrewdly.

But then Jesus says, "Whoever can be trusted with little can also be trusted with much, and whoever is dishonest with very little will also be dishonest with much. So if you have not been trustworthy in handling worldly wealth, who will trust you with true riches? And if you have not been trustworthy with someone else's property, who will give you property of your own?" (vv. 10–12).

God calls us to be faithful when it comes to money. Bill, a salesman I know, routinely "fudged" on his income taxes and lied to customers. Then he started attending a men's Bible study and began meeting other men like himself. As they studied God's Word together and shared their stories, God convicted Bill that he was not trustworthy handling the money he did have or the interests of his customers. Bill repented, and he has started his own small business, which over the last several years, is flourishing. He became faithful with little, and God has given him much. He became faithful with what belonged to others, and God gave him his own.

There are lots of Bible verses on wealth, but none is more central to the biblical perspective than Luke 16:13. It says, "No servant can serve two masters. Either he will hate the one and love the other, or he will be devoted to the one and despise the other. You cannot serve both God and Money."

Money is a great servant but a ruthless master. That's the big idea of this chapter. As the Scripture simply explains, you cannot serve both God and money. You will grow to love one and hate the other.

The starting place to understand God's view of wealth is to see it as His gift. The Bible repeatedly declares God is the source of all money that we have:

But remember the Lord your God, for it is he who gives you the ability to produce wealth, and so confirms his covenant, which he swore to your forefathers. (Deuteronomy 8:18)

Wealth and honor come from you; you are the ruler of all things. In your hands are strength and power to exalt and give strength to all. (1 Chronicles 29:12)

Moreover, when God gives any man wealth and possessions, and enables him to enjoy them, to accept his lot and be happy in his work—this is a gift of God. (Ecclesiastes 5:19)

The Perils of Money Love

Money is a gift from God, but it comes with perils and disappointments. The Bible says if you love money, you will forfeit contentment:

Whoever loves money never has money enough; whoever loves wealth is never satisfied with his income. This too is meaningless. As goods increase, so do those who consume them. And what benefit are they to the owner except to feast his eyes on them? The sleep of a laborer is sweet, whether he eats little or much, but the abundance of a rich man permits him no sleep. (Ecclesiastes 5:10–12)

Once you get above a certain level, money creates more problems than it solves. For example, when I had ten employees, life was good. I knew each of them well. I knew their spouses and the names of their children. I had a great income, a beautiful home, nice clothes, a good car, delicious meals, wonderful kids, and a fantastic wife.

Later, when I had one hundred employees, the money was considerably more. However, I didn't know everyone who worked for me—much less their spouses and children.

When you have ten employees, there are forty-five total possible relationships (n times [n minus 1] divided by 2). With one hundred employees, the number of potential relationships and interactions goes up exponentially. A tenfold increase in staff resulted in 4,950 possible relationships! So suddenly, we needed an entire administrative department just to keep track of people. They didn't actually "make" or "contribute" anything to the bottom line!

> **YOU CANNOT SERVE BOTH GOD AND MONEY. YOU WILL SERVE ONLY THE ONE YOU LOVE.**

But here's the interesting thing. I was living in the same home, wearing the same clothes, driving the same car, and eating the same meals. However, I was more stressed, and that affected how much emotional energy was left at the end of the day to bring home to my fantastic wife and wonderful kids.

By contrast, in his letter to his spiritual son Timothy, the apostle Paul explained, "Godliness with contentment is great gain. For we brought nothing into the world, and we can take nothing out of it. But if we have food and clothing, we will be content with that." And as a spiritual father, Paul also reminded Timothy, "People who want to get rich fall into temptation and a trap and into many foolish and harmful desires that plunge men into ruin and destruction. For the love of money is a root of all kinds of evil. Some people, eager for money, have wandered from the faith and pierced themselves with many griefs" (1 Timothy 6:6–10).

Andrew Carnegie was right when he said, "Millionaires who laugh are rare, very rare indeed."

That is the peril of wealth. In our culture, we need to have money. When the mortgage payment comes due, your lender is not looking for Jesus. He wants cash! But above a certain level, money can create more problems than it solves. When wealth competes with God in your priorities so that money becomes your master, you are on the road to ruin.

You cannot serve both God and Money. You will serve only the one you love.

Money Love = Success Sickness

Jesus told a parable about spreading seeds that landed in four very different places. The first seeds fell on a pathway and never had a chance to sprout because the ground was too hard, and the birds came and ate the seeds. The second batch of seeds fell into rocky soil and sprang up quickly, but then died because the roots couldn't penetrate the stones. The third seeds fell among weeds and thorns and had to compete for nutrients, so they withered. But the fourth batch of seeds fell on fertile and well-prepared soil, so they thrived.

Jesus explained the parable to His disciples, and in Matthew 13:22 we find His explanation for the third seed that fell among thorns. He said this represents "the man who hears the word, but the worries of this life and the deceitfulness of wealth choke it, making it unfruitful."

If you're like me, you understand the futility of living among the thorns. I remember when I was a teenager, sitting in the kitchen and telling my parents that I was going to be a millionaire. That became an internal value within my worldview—"Money will solve my problems, and success will make me happy." It attached itself to me as part of my identity, and it became a driving force in my life. Then I became a Christian.

At first, my new spiritual birth didn't change this area of my life. I still was consumed by the "worries of this life and the deceitfulness of wealth." It never dawned on me that I needed to surrender my youthful ambition. I simply wasn't spiritually mature enough to know that money-love and God-love oppose each other. I started to love God, but I continued to love money. I lived that way for a decade. Then one day I looked around and noticed that some of the other guys in my sphere of influence were getting a different result from their Christianity than I was. You see, that's the last part of Jesus' description of people who try to live among the thorns—the worries of life "choke [the seed], making [their lives] unfruitful."

I called a timeout. I thought I would spend a couple of weeks figuring this out. Instead, I spent the next two and a half years "staring at my navel," as it were, not understanding the issues that were robbing me of spiritual vitality and fruitfulness. One day, as I was reading my Bible, that's when I discovered Matthew 13:22, about the seed that fell among the thorns. I said, "That's my life! The deceitfulness of wealth . . . I've been deceived!"

I humbled myself and repented of that lifestyle. I had a disease we might call "success sickness." *Success sickness is the disease of always wanting more, but never being happy when we get it.* For me, failure wasn't about not getting what I wanted—I did. For me, failure was to succeed in a way that doesn't really matter.

Before God opened my eyes to the deceitfulness of wealth, I told myself, "In order to be happy, I must have money." Then God began to reshape my life. Money is morally neutral, so its perils and disappointments are not innate. The danger, however, is in how we relate to it. It never satisfies. It promises freedom, but it enslaves. Accumulation leaves a bitter aftertaste of futility and boredom. The problem with money is that it makes promises it cannot keep.

When Money Is Your Master

How can you tell if you are trying to serve two masters? Actually, it may not be as easy as you would think. The Old Testament prophet Jeremiah noted, "The heart is deceitful above all things. . . . Who can understand it?" (Jeremiah 17:9). Demosthenes put it this way: "Nothing is easier than self-deceit, for what each man wishes that he also believes to be true." So, even as Christians, we can deceive ourselves about the true nature of our relationship with God and with money.

Let me offer five money-love scenarios to help you determine which master you're really serving. The basic idea for all of these scenarios is simple. You can know that money is your master if wealth is your goal.

Scenario #1: "I can handle it"

You're a Christian, but you really want to be rich. You say to yourself, "I can handle being wealthy." That amounts to nothing more than positive self-talk.

I challenge you to pray, "In my heart, I truly don't know if I can handle it, or if I'll ever be able to handle it. So God, deal graciously with me, and help me to trust You to provide in the way that will never disconnect me from loving You first."

Scenario #2: "Money will solve my problems"

You are facing a problem, and you believe money will solve it. This is one of the great myths of all time. If you're not happy where you are, you will not be happy where you want to be. The secret of contentment is not in having what you want—it's in wanting what you have.

I challenge you to believe in the supreme wisdom of a gracious God who is able to work all things for your benefit—even the things that look bad now.

Scenario #3: "I can't be happy with less than _____ dollars"

You really believe you can't be happy without *x* amount of dollars. Perhaps you don't realize you're actually saying that Jesus is not enough—you need something more. Consider the biblical record of a rich young man who came to Jesus, asking what he needed to gain eternal life. He had lived a moral life, but Jesus said he should sell everything, give the money to the poor, and follow Him. Scripture says the man "went away sad, because he had great wealth" (Mark 10:22).

Wealth won't give you joy—only Jesus can do that.

Scenario #4: You wear yourself out to make money

You find yourself working more and more hours, not because you are lacking, but because you want more. Solomon, the richest man in the world, advised,

"Do not wear yourself out to get rich; have the wisdom to show restraint. Cast but a glance at riches, and they are gone, for they will surely sprout wings and fly off to the sky like an eagle" (Proverbs 23:4–5).

If you are wearing yourself out to make money, you can be pretty sure you are caught up in money-love.

Scenario #5: You hoard your money and are not charitable

Instead of being charitable, you are hoarding your money. Jesus told a parable about a man whose crops did very well. In essence, you could say he had a big return on an investment. Instead of sharing his gain, he built bigger barns (investment portfolio) to store it. God said to him, "You fool! This very night your life will be demanded from you." And the parable concludes with this statement: "This is how it will be with anyone who stores up things for himself but is not rich toward God" (Luke 12:20–21).

How can you know if you have it wrong? Money is your master when wealth is your goal.

When Money Is Your Servant

Leaving Our Future in God's Hands

We've said repeatedly that money is a great servant, but it's a ruthless master. We've discussed how you can gauge whether money is your master. But how can you know you're getting it right? How can you know that money is your servant rather than your master?

You know you have it right if you can leave your future in God's hands and say, "If it is His will." The book of James explains it like this: "Now listen, you who say, 'Today or tomorrow we will go to this or that city, spend a year there, carry on business and make money.' Why, you do not even know what will happen tomorrow. What is your life? You are a mist that appears for a little while and then vanishes. Instead, you ought to say, 'If it is the Lord's will, we will live and do this or that'" (James 4:13–15).

Escaping the Pride of Prosperity

You also know you have it right if you can agree with the prayer of Agur found in Proverbs 30:7–9. Once I realized I had success sickness, I remember reading this prayer and wanting to imitate Agur and escape from the snare of materialism. Agur said, "Two things I ask of you, O Lord; do not refuse me before I die: Keep falsehood and lies far from me; give me neither poverty nor riches, but give me only my daily bread. Otherwise, I may have too much and disown you and say, 'Who is the Lord?' Or I may become poor and steal, and so dishonor the name of my God."

Agur prayed to escape the pride of prosperity—having too much and disowning God. Who in their right mind would want to put themselves in that kind of jeopardy? Scripture does not require you to pray in agreement with Agur. But if you chafe at the idea, you may want to do some soul-searching to determine which master you are serving, God or money. If you don't chafe at the prayer, then you probably have it right.

I know people who are so wealthy that they can spend without thinking about it. I'm blessed, but not that blessed! In fact, I've gone from wanting to be a skizillionaire to being terrified at the thought of being wealthy. At one point in my life I had so much, but I was on the verge of losing everything. When God was dismantling my personal empire, I could tell what my friends were thinking: "Wow, I don't know what he's done but he must be under God's curse." But it was not a curse; it was a blessing. God was removing the shakable kingdom—created things—to make room for the unshakable kingdom. The curse is in having all that stuff and still not being happy.

Getting It Right

You know you are getting it right . . .

- when you are content with what you have right now.
- when you are rich toward God, regardless of your financial circumstances.
- when you are generous and charitable.
- if you would have no hesitation to let a fellow Christian look at your checkbook.

- when you can say that money is your servant, and wealth is the by-product of bringing glory to God.

Remember "the main thing" that is always happening? God is sovereignly orchestrating all of the seemingly random circumstances of your life to bring you into right relationship with Him and right relationship with other people.

If He wants you to have wealth, nothing you do will prevent it. If He does not want you to have wealth, no amount of begging will change His mind. You will never honestly make one dollar more or one dollar less than God wants you to make. In the end, you can find comfort and contentment in the sovereignty and goodness of our great God.

Servant or Master?

So, after careful examination, can you say that money is your servant? Or is it your master?

For the first twenty-four years of my life, money was my master. Then I spent another fourteen years trying to have the best of both worlds. In despair, I prayed the prayer of Agur, and I found that God was pleased to answer. If you want to inoculate yourself from wealth's perils and disappointments, you may want to pray the prayer too. God will be faithful to honor your desire.

A PRAYER YOU CAN PRAY

This prayer comes from Agur in Proverbs 30:7–9:

Two things I ask of you, O Lord; do not refuse me before I die: Keep falsehood and lies far from me; give me neither poverty nor riches, but give me only my daily bread. Otherwise, I may have too much and disown you and say, "Who is the Lord?" Or I may become poor and steal, and so dishonor the name of my God. Amen.

Questions for Personal Reflection
or Group Discussion

1. Have you handled money well or not? Give an example.

2. Which of this chapter's biblical principles most attracted your attention and why?

   Luke 16:8–13

   1 Timothy 6:6–10

   Ecclesiastes 5:10–12

   Proverbs 23:4–5

   Proverbs 30:7–9

   James 4:13–15

3. What is your goal for money? Is money your master or servant, and why?

8

Temporal **WORK** as a **KINGDOM** Priority

ONE OF THE BENEFITS OF TRAVELING is building a portfolio of good stories. Unfortunately, most of those stories are about the challenges of traveling.

I remember, for instance, a flight that stopped at the Shreveport, Louisiana, airport. The first person in my security check looked at my picture ID. She examined it carefully, looked at me, looked back at the card, and took the time to tell me the date that my license would expire.

Then I came to the line of people waiting to have their luggage checked. A man was helping passengers put their items on the conveyor belt before the metal detector. He asked if I was carrying any hazardous substances.

"No sir."

He continued, "Are you carrying any weapons?" And we went through a dozen similar questions. Then he turned to my sweet wife and asked her the same things.

After his interrogation, we went through the metal detector. We had to remove everything that was not made of fabric. Then they pulled my wife out of the line and took her to a different location, where a female security guard went through every item in Patsy's purse and cosmetic case.

I said, "Wow, this is amazing! Is there some big military installation or a drug traffic drop-off in this area? What is so important that there are such top security measures?"

A security official said, "Really, we don't have that much traffic, so there just isn't much else to do."

In another instance, I was departing Orlando when I got "tagged" in the security line for additional screening.

"Why do you do that?" I asked, as a security official swabbed my bags.

"We're testing for explosives."

"Really? I always thought you used that to test for drugs," I said.

He said, "We used to, but we don't care about that anymore."

For most of us, our lives are more like the Orlando airport. We're too busy to check every little detail. We live at a hectic pace, balancing a heavy load of demands from family, church, friends, work, charitable organizations, and recreation. Add economic pressures, and many of us are out of bandwidth. We have to prioritize.

What Are Priorities, and Why Do They Matter?

Everyone lives by priorities. Basically, a priority is something to which we assign a degree of importance or urgency. When we prioritize, we arrange items or tasks by their order of importance. That process matters because, frankly, if I don't decide what is important for me, someone else will.

Jesus is our model for setting priorities in business and life. Jesus was the undisputed rock star of His day. People mobbed Him. Sometimes He was so overwhelmed by people that He didn't even have time to eat, the Bible says. They wouldn't even let Him pray in peace.

When Jesus' popularity was growing, Luke 4:42–44 says,

At daybreak Jesus went out to a solitary place. The people were looking for him and when they came to where he was, they tried to keep him from leaving them. But he said, "I must preach the good news of the kingdom of God to the other towns also, because that is why I was sent." And he kept on preaching in the synagogues of Judea.

Jesus made His decisions on the basis of His priorities, not His pressures. He knew His calling, His "reason for living." That helped Him understand what was important and what wasn't. And because of that, Jesus said no to the people who wanted Him to change His plan—even though what they wanted wasn't a bad thing. Jesus just had a different reason for living.

The big idea for this chapter is this: *When compared to nonbelievers, my priorities as a Christian are motivated by an altogether different reason for living.* My purpose is wrapped up in growing God's kingdom and tending His culture—not building my empire. And my list of priorities—the guiding principles that help me decide where to invest time and energy—should reflect that difference.

Work is a high priority. For Christians, however, work is one among a plethora of priorities. Of course, lots of Christians get the work priority out of whack. We may see ourselves as defined by our work—career advancement, whether within the company or by taking a new job somewhere else, is our priority. There's nothing wrong with wanting to develop our skills and being the best we can at what we do. But that should not be our top priority. Yet many of us are tempted to give our job top billing. That's probably because it takes up the single largest block of our time.

Jesus Defined Our Reason for Living

Understanding our purpose is one of the crucial issues in determining priorities. Earlier in this book, we examined purpose as it relates to work. But now, we're going to look a little more deeply at Jesus' teachings on the subject. Let's examine a number of verses that draw a general picture of why and how we should live.

Living to Have and Share the Abundant Life

Let's start with Jesus' declaration in the Gospel of John, which records Jesus saying, "The thief comes only to steal and kill and destroy; I have come that they may have life, and have it to the full" (John 10:10).

Our reason for living is to receive abundant life from Jesus. There are many aspects to this, but that overarching principle should affect all our decisions— personal and professional. When you answer the phone at work or have a conversation with a coworker, you should intend to give and receive God's blessings, so you can serve and bring glory to God by your actions. Sure, you're trying to complete a project. But bigger things are happening than just finishing a job— God is working all things for His glory. Remember, the sovereign, supreme ruler of all creation is interested in the outcome of that telephone call, that meeting, or that deadline. Without God, a person does not have that assurance.

Do you see how the Christian worldview is utterly different from that of the skeptic? If your sense of purpose is limited to making a profit, you'll eventually find it's a puny, tepid reason for living. Once you've known the glories and riches of God's kingdom, how could you ever settle for mere profit?

Turning Our Value System Upside Down

The abundant life provides a much greater reason for living, but it also turns our value system upside down. Our natural tendency is to seek personal gain. But Jesus walked a very different road. Even though Jesus is one with the Father, in His humanity He "did not consider equality with God something to be grasped, but made himself nothing, taking the very nature of a servant, being made in human likeness. And being found in appearance as a man, he humbled himself and became obedient to death—even death on a cross" (Philippians 2:6–8).

By personal experience, Jesus understood self-denial. Through His example and through His words, He taught His disciples—including us—to value things of eternal consequence over temporal pleasure and gain. And He calls His followers to live by the priorities He demonstrated when He lived on earth. To all His followers, He says, "If anyone would come after me, he must deny himself and take up his cross and follow me. For whoever wants to save his life will lose it, but who-

INTERESTINGLY, THE MARKETPLACE TENDS TO REWARD PEOPLE FOR LIVING BY BIBLICAL STANDARDS.

ever loses his life for me will find it. What good will it be for a man if he gains the whole world, yet forfeits his soul? Or what can a man give in exchange for his soul?" (Matthew 16:24–26).

He tells us, "Seek first his kingdom and his righteousness, and all these things will be given to you as well" (Matthew 6:33). We are not limited by the "ceiling" of temporal living. We have a higher purpose—to seek His kingdom and His righteousness.

Harmonizing Kingdom and Workplace Priorities

Participating in the workforce does not put you at war with Christian values. Interestingly enough, the marketplace tends to reward people for living by biblical standards. The work world prizes character traits like integrity, diligence, excellence, honesty, and humility.

Being Productive in Order to Honor God

So, what's the primary difference between a Christian worker and a nonbelieving worker? For a non-Christian, these positive traits are a means to an end—they bring monetary reward, or they contribute to community image and public relations. For the Christian, they are ends in themselves. Because a believer seeks God's kingdom, he lives in a way that reflects righteousness. The difference is the motivation and the establishment of priorities.

Christians and non-Christians both want to be productive. I can't imagine anyone choosing to go into the workforce without that desire. But Christians have a specific motivation. Jesus told His disciples, "This is to my Father's glory, that you bear much fruit, showing yourselves to be my disciples" (John 15:8). Fruitfulness—or being productive—is for the Christian not an end in itself. It's a means to reflect God's character to the world and to bring Him glory.

In some ways, this chapter brings us "full circle," because at its most basic level, this whole book is about priorities. Each chapter features a topic that influences how people prioritize. If you see work as a calling, as we discussed in chapter 1, you will establish priorities reflecting that viewpoint. Those priorities will drive your daily decisions.

Loyalty to the Family

For example, entrepreneur and Christian author Bob Buford understands the importance of priorities. Bob was chairman of the board and CEO of Buford Television, Inc. His family-owned business started with a single ABC affiliate in Texas and eventually grew to become a network of cable systems that stretched across the country.

Bob sold his company to devote the "second half" of his life to, among other things, helping people successfully navigate the second half of life. If you read Buford's books, or books or articles about him, it becomes clear he has had a profound impact on the way people think about their lives as believers in business. For him, being a businessman is the same thing as being a minister.

At age forty-eight, Bob listed a few key life goals. His top priority was "to walk worthy of my calling." And he had two other priorities to help him succeed: "To have a primary loyalty to Jesus Christ" and "To make one person happy"—his wife, Linda. Bob then developed a twenty-one-year plan designed to help him achieve his priorities.

Entrepreneur Jeff McWaters also understands biblical priorities. Jeff founded Amerigroup to provide healthcare services for the financially vulnerable, seniors, and people with disabilities. In a few short years the company grew to 2,600 employees. Most of their contracts are with government agencies. Here are Jeff's priorities in his own words: "First, that my kids would know that I am a man who is just as trustworthy in business as at home and, second, that in my business career I would never be asked to do something unethical, because people know I would never even consider it."[1]

Loyalty to Your Coworkers

Throughout this book, we've also discussed how Christians in the workplace are called to behave toward people. Jack Alexander, CEO of Geronimo Investments, described a time when his company's biggest client badly mistreated his staff. As a priority, Jack clearly believed that people are more important than profit, so he made an appointment with the executive team representing that customer. He told them, "You are by far our largest client, but your people are going to have to stop mistreating my people, or we will drop you."[2]

Jack's willingness to act on his priority automatically set him apart from the unbelieving world, and it reflected well on his God. Fortunately, they retained the client, but it could just have easily gone the other way.

Proper Priorities: Good for the Bottom Line

Delegating Authority

Skip Ast, president of pool and spa maker Shasta Industries, told me, "In my infancy stages, I did everything. I came to the warehouse early in the morning to get the equipment. I went out and laid the pools, or supervised them. I even collected the money at night. But there came a time—because God was growing this thing so rapidly—that I was working myself to death."

Skip had to establish priorities, and he looked for people in his organization whom he could trust to assume responsibilities that he had been handling on his own. "I asked this guy to take over a position I'd been doing in the field. He said he would—that he had just been waiting for me to ask. I relinquished that, and I just stayed away." The man did such a great job that, in a follow-up interview, the customer told Skip he was "astonished," because the project exceeded his expectations.

Noting that Shasta has built a solid reputation by continually striving to "astonish" customers, Skip concluded, "That's where I want to keep this company. So far we've been the number one leading builder—by the grace of God. This will be our fortieth consecutive year, something nobody else has done. That all comes from God's grace and putting our priorities in order."[3]

Praying about a Specific Task

My friend Os Hillman sent me an article about an attorney from Nigeria who had occasion to argue a case before the Supreme Court of his country. Just before the hearing, the attorney assembled his staff and wife in the chambers, and they prayed about the case. He had five points, but after they had prayed, he said God told him not to argue points one through four of the complaint.

This lawyer just obeyed God. When the court convened, he approached the judge and said he wanted to amend his plea. He wanted to drop the first four counts, and he would prefer only to argue the fifth.

The judge was shocked but granted permission. The other attorney got up, but for twelve minutes he could not complete a sentence. Finally in utter frustration he approached the bench and said, "Your honor, it is unfortunate that [the opposing attorney] is not arguing the first four points. I am forced to yield my case."

The attorney who obeyed God's direction won, because the other lawyer prepared a response for the first four counts, but he had nothing for the fifth. This is the advantage of allowing God's Holy Spirit to invade your work.

"Live by Biblical Priorities"

Bill Walton, cofounder of Holiday Inns, just about ruined his life by getting his priorities mixed up. One morning, after listening to several men from thirty-five to forty-five years of age speak about their spiritual journeys, Walton stood up and spoke: "It is true that I helped build one of America's great corporations. But in order to do so I arrived at the office every morning by seven and rarely got home before ten o'clock at night." His posture drooped, and then he added with a quivering lip, "I never saw a single Little League baseball game, and now my children don't want to talk to me."

He paused and stared sadly into their faces as though he could see the future. He took a deep breath to gather himself. Then, with trembling fists and booming voice, his words echoed through the room: "I exhort you, young men. Don't let that happen to you. Learn to live by biblical priorities!"[4]

As Christians, our priorities are reflected in our daily decisions and in our behavior. If our priorities are in alignment with God's Word and His way, we will be set apart from skeptics, because we will be motivated by an altogether different reason for living. We will focus on glorifying God through our work.

A PRAYER YOU CAN PRAY

Lord Jesus, You are awesome. Thank You so much that, because we have an eternal view through Your Word, we don't have a temporal ceiling. Our thoughts can range to the outer reaches of the cosmos, and even beyond that, into the holy of holies. We can bring You with us into our meetings. We can pray and make plans by seeking Your counsel. Lord, we can set our priorities differently from our unbelieving acquaintances, because we have this altogether different reason for living.

I ask Your blessing as I seek to prioritize my life based on the principles of Your Word. I ask this in the powerful name of Jesus, amen.

Questions for Personal Reflection
or Group Discussion

1. What are the important things a Christian might do in work that would be different from what a non-Christian might do? What important things might be the same?

2. Read Luke 4:42–44. Imagine that you are Jesus. People are begging you not to leave. What is going through your mind? Why don't you stay? How do you decide?

3. What are your work priorities, or what would you like them to be? How do you decide? Pick one, and over the next week think about how to apply it each day.

9

PRAYER:

Is It **OKAY** to
Pray for **SUCCESS?**

GIVEN THE FAMINES, FLOODS, and disasters that ravage people, shouldn't we feel at least a little guilty or uncomfortable praying for success at work? Given the sacrifices made by missionaries and relief workers, isn't it a little self-centered to ask God for a blessing as an employee or business owner?

Compared to devastating circumstances in other people's lives—such as joblessness, cancer, aging parents, poverty, and wayward children—success seems to barely rank as a prayer need. In fact, praying for success sometimes seems downright selfish.

Our appeal, however, is not to human wisdom but to God's Word, which all but begs us to pray about *everything*. The Bible never guarantees success, as some proclaim, but we are encouraged to pray for peace and prosperity, and God hears and grants every prayer in accordance with His will. To the exiles in Babylon, God said, "Also, seek the peace and prosperity of the city to which I have carried you into exile. Pray to the Lord for it, because if it prospers, you too will prosper" (Jeremiah 29:7).

Actually, one of God's best methods for helping victims of famines, floods, disasters, joblessness, cancer, and poverty is to surround them with some success.

So, in this chapter, we're going to look at what the Bible has to say about praying for success in three specific workplace situations:

- prayer for the success of a specific idea
- prayer for the success of a specific task
- prayer for success against a specific threat

Praying for a Specific Idea

Nehemiah's Prayer

The Old Testament records a period when many Israelites were exiled to Babylon. Nehemiah was one of those exiles; his new employer was no less than King Artaxerxes of Persia. Nehemiah served as cupbearer to the king. By today's understanding, that might not sound like an important job. But it would have been similar to being a cabinet member—an advisor to the king.

Nehemiah's story opens with a visit from his brother Hanani and some other visitors from Judah. They told him the people back in their homeland were in great trouble and disgrace. Jerusalem's walls had been compromised, and the city was in disarray.

Nehemiah's response was to weep, to mourn, to fast, and to pray. He confessed Israel's sins and noted that Moses had warned how God would scatter the Israelites if they disobeyed Him. But Moses also had said that even during any exile, if the people would return to God and obey His commands, God would bring them home again.

Then Nehemiah requested, "O Lord, let your ear be attentive to the prayer of this your servant and to the prayers of your servants who delight in revering your name. Give your servant success today by granting him favor in the presence of this man" (Nehemiah 1:11).

Basically, Nehemiah was saying, "God, I have an idea that I believe is within

Your will. Please give me success." Then he watched for an opportunity to approach the king.

One day, as he was serving wine, the king noticed the change in his cupbearer's demeanor. "Why are you so sad?" he asked. Nehemiah explained the report he had received from his brother, and the king basically asked, "What is it that you want?"

The Bible says that Nehemiah paused to pray before answering, and then he shared his idea with the king: "If it pleases the king and if your servant has found favor in his sight, let him send me to the city in Judah where my fathers are buried so that I can rebuild it" (2:5).

That was his vision—a specific task—to rebuild Jerusalem. He had prayed for success. And God answered graciously. Nehemiah wrote, "Because the gracious hand of my God was upon me, the king granted my requests" (Nehemiah 2:8b).

Our Dependence on God

Nehemiah's story illustrates this principle: The God who gives visions will also fulfill those visions through men who pray in humble dependence on their Lord's power and might.

If God gives you an idea, you can pray for its success.

Hudson Taylor, the great nineteenth-century English missionary to China, once explained, "Many Christians estimate difficulties in the light of their own resources, and thus attempt little and often fail in the little they attempt. All God's giants have been weak men, who did great things for God because they reckoned on His power and presence being with them."

Here's the big idea of this chapter: *Prayer releases the power of God into the mundane affairs of our daily lives.*

Prayer at Interstate Batteries

Norm Miller, chairman of Interstate Batteries, understands the power of praying for a specific idea. At one point while his company was establishing its brand, several competitors mimicked Interstate's system of signing distributors, gas stations, and garages. Then some of these competitors decided to host conventions.

Norm said, "We had never done that, but decided we should—in Hawaii.

We had no idea what we were doing. What if we blew it? We sat down and talked about it and decided to pray that God would make us successful. We made a list and wrote down all we thought was important, everything that we wanted God to do, and we began meeting every morning at nine, and we prayed through the list for eighteen months."

When they got to the convention, interesting things began to happen. One person said, "What is going on here? I feel love here. What's the deal?" One of Norm Miller's specific prayers was that people would feel God's love at the convention. One woman said, "I go to fifteen conventions a year. I have never been to anything like this before. I don't understand it."[1]

Someone came up with the term "the Interstate family," and it has stuck ever since. The distributors of Interstate batteries consider themselves part of the Interstate family. That is the power of prayer—a leader's prayer that true love would be felt when distributors met together.

So what is your idea? Like Nehemiah, does it fill you with passion? Does it also make you a little sad? Are you afraid it won't work out? Is it taking longer than you expected? Jesus tells us, "If you remain in me and my words remain in you, ask whatever you wish, and it will be given you" (John 15:7). If your idea is from God, failure to pray for success would be to dishonor Him.

Praying for a Specific Task

Abraham was very old. His wife, Sarah, had already died, and he was nearing the end of his life. The Bible says, "The Lord had blessed him in every way" (Genesis 24:1). Clearly, though, one thing was bothering this patriarch—his son Isaac did not yet have a wife.

The Task of Abraham's Servant

Abraham called his chief servant and made him promise to find Isaac a wife—not a Canaanite woman from the surrounding area, but a woman from the homeland of Abraham's birth. He asked his servant to "swear by the Lord, the God of heaven and the God of earth, that you will . . . go to my country and my own relatives and get a wife for my son Isaac" (Genesis 24:3–4).

This faithful servant went to a town called Nahor. As he was resting and watering his camels, he prayed: "O Lord, God of my master Abraham, give me success today, and show kindness to my master, Abraham" (Genesis 24:12). This was a prayer for the success of a specific task.

There at the watering well he met Rebekah, who was related to Abraham. The girl's family agreed to release her, Rebekah agreed to go, and Abraham's servant fulfilled his mission.

Thank God that's an assignment you'll never have to fulfill! But you might be given responsibility for a project or a sale, starting a business, doing a repair. Maybe you'll have a challenging deadline. Or maybe you'll be asked to do something that seems too big. This biblical example demonstrates that you can pray specifically for success in accomplishing your assignment. Jesus has invited us to pray about anything and everything.

The Task of Interstate Batteries' Miller

Early in the life of Interstate Batteries, Norm Miller prayed, "God, please take our advertising and promotion money and multiply it beyond any expectations."

Miller notes, "Within a year and a half, a headline in *Consumer Reports* said, 'Of all the batteries tested, one stood out above the rest.'" It was Interstate. But Miller adds, "The wild thing was, it was a bad test! It wasn't fair because they had made a mistake."

About the same time, a couple in Milwaukee, Wisconsin, were driving in a rainstorm. They lost control of their car, and it careened into a lake. They were unharmed, but the next day—twenty-four hours later—when the wrecker came to pull the car out of the water, the windshield wipers and lights were still on.

Radio commentator Paul Harvey reported the outcome on his national broadcast. "Wow! That's some kind of battery!" he said. "I wonder what it was?" And Harvey was deluged with calls from people who also wanted to know. So he poked around, and the next day he talked about it again. And he told his listeners the battery was made by Interstate Batteries.

"We got unbelievable response," Norm said, "and that was also after we had done this praying. And we ended up advertising with Paul Harvey for ten years. That was our first major advertising expenditure. He reached five million people, and they were really loyal to his products."[2]

For Interstate, the specific task was to wisely use its advertising and marketing budget—to multiply it and bring the company success. Whatever the task, we should pray that we accomplish it with great success.

I think a lot of us are not aggressive enough in pursuing and praying for success. Many men have a false guilt and uncertainty and a certain discomfort with success that is simply not found in the Bible.

> ## TO NOT PRAY FOR SUCCESS IS TO DISHONOR GOD.

Let's learn a lesson from Norm Miller. To not pray for success is to dishonor God.

Praying About a Specific Threat

King David against the Philistines

Finally, let's look at David, a man who prayed for success when he faced a specific threat. The Philistines didn't like David very much. Who can blame them, since he killed their fiercest warrior when David was just a teenager? Years later, when the Philistines heard that David had become king, they came out in full force to attack. They spread themselves out in the valley of Rephaim.

In the face of this threat, notice that David's first response was to seek God's guidance. He prayed, "Shall I go and attack the Philistines? Will you hand them over to me?" (2 Samuel 5:19).

In our work, we all face threats. I remember speaking in a small town in Minnesota. A nationally known retail giant had recently established a huge store at the edge of the city. The downtown area was dust. Those shop owners weren't under military attack like David was, but they faced a threat to their survival. Your "threat" will be different, but when you're in trouble like that, what should you do? The same thing David did—pray.

David inquired of the Lord, "Shall I go and attack the Philistines? Will you hand them over to me?"

And God answered, "Go, for I will surely hand the Philistines over to you" (2 Samuel 5:19). David obeyed, and God honored His promise. David defeated the Philistines.

Seeking Direction When a Specific Threat Arises

When you are having a David moment, facing a specific threat to your livelihood, I challenge you to pray—especially when you think you already know what to do. Whether the threat is downsizing, and you want to prove your worth to the boss so your position doesn't get cut, or it's the ability to remain physically and mentally sharp when you feel fatigued, pray for the Lord to show you the right action to take.

On another occasion, the Philistines came again to the same valley. David could have simply attacked the same way, with the very same strategy, and assumed that God would again grant victory. That's probably what most of us would do. But David didn't do that. Instead, he again sought direction from God—and this time God gave him a *different* plan:

> So David inquired of the Lord, and he answered, "Do not go straight up, but circle around behind them and attack them in front of the balsam trees. As soon as you hear the sound of marching in the tops of the balsam trees, move quickly, because that will mean the Lord has gone out in front of you to strike the Philistine army." So David did as the Lord commanded him, and he struck down the Philistines. (2 Samuel 5:23–25)

Sometimes God will give specific directions, sometimes not. But when we pray for help in dealing with a specific threat, we honor God. Whether a laborer or a manager, you will find God wants to hear and respond to the threats you face.

Specific Prayer for a Specific Threat at a Pool Company

In the work world, we don't face armed enemies like David did. But Skip Ast can tell you the threats are still real. In 1967, he left a comfortable position as general manager for a pool company to join his brother Bob, working for a home builder who had decided to install pools in new homes. He took a 35 percent pay reduction in the process.

Skip and his wife had "survival money" to cover about two months, and the company owner committed to provide the start-up money for the new venture. Skip remembered, "Within a week after my arrival, the owner told Bob he was throwing in the towel on this pool division thing, and if I couldn't make it go in two weeks, he was shutting it down. Bob came to me with that, and then he actually had a heart attack, and I had to put him in the hospital—which left me to deal with a stranger."

Skip went home and told his wife. Then he talked to God. "Lord, we've prayed about this," he said. "My wife is disappointed, but we are trusting You. How do You want me to handle this whole thing?"

After he finished praying, Skip began to develop a newspaper ad. He visited the builder the following morning, and they ran the ad on Friday night and Saturday morning.

Skip explained what happened next. "To use the expression from Malachi, God just 'opened the windows of heaven and poured out' more leads than we could handle. In no time, we had enough business, and with cash flow developing, I could see I had his confidence, and we were rapidly moving ahead."

The company gained so much business that, for about eighteen months, Skip regularly worked from 4 a.m. till 8 or 9 p.m. He made time to be with his family every day, and especially on weekends. But he said, "God gave me such supernatural strength that I never tired, and at the end of seven months, we had built 230 pools. By the end of 1968, we had built 550 and had become the number one builder in Arizona. God continued to bless the business that way, and we kept growing."

Today, Skip is president of Shasta Industries, the largest independent pool builder internationally, and he says, "There is never a day that goes by that we don't pray and commit this business to God."

Prayer Practicalities

Suppose you are competing against others to purchase a piece of property. You settle all the details with the seller, and you're about to sign the contract. Then a competitor shows up. Do you rely on your own competence, experience, and determination? In some sense, you might know what to do. Even so, you need to pray, especially when you think you know what to do. God may tell you you're right, or He may give you a different plan altogether.

Remember, regardless of the outcome, when we fail to pray for success, we dishonor God. In work, prayer is not just important—it's mandatory. Prayer is our goal. Now let's look at three practicalities that will help us realize that goal.

1. Spend Time with God Every Day

In many places, Scripture tells us to pray often—without ceasing, on all occasions, and with all kinds of prayers and requests (Ephesians 6:18; Philippians 4:6; Colossians 1:9; 4:2; 1 Thessalonians 5:17). What does that look like in real life? I know two businessmen who are good friends. They talk on the phone several times each day. I've heard them, so I know there is a familiarity in their conversation and a certain brotherly affection in their voices. I'm pretty good friends with them, but I only talk with them once a week or less. I have a very different relationship with them than they have with each other.

It is the same way with our Lord and Savior Jesus Christ. If you only talk with Him every now and then, you won't have the same relationship as someone who talks with Him several times a day. You should try to keep a close relationship with Him.

2. Make a List

Make a list of things you believe will contribute to your success. Then make an appointment—a specific time every day, when you pray through your list. That could be a lifelong commitment to pray over broad goals, or it could be a short-term commitment to pray over a specific project.

Commit to this, and try to be consistent.

3. Get a Resource

Find a book, video, article, or workbook on prayer. Learn more about God's Word on prayer, and find out what Christian thinkers have said through the years.

A PRAYER YOU CAN PRAY

Father, this spiritual discipline of prayer has been the chief business of Your great saints throughout the ages. I ask that You would make it my chief business too. Help me to recognize that prayer is a conversation with You, back and forth, so that by this conversation a precious salvation also becomes a close relationship. Please encourage me to sit regularly with You through prayer.

Give me the conviction that prayer is the most powerful and efficient investment of time. Whatever I encounter, good or bad, may my automatic response be to pray. I ask this in Your wonderful and powerful name, amen.

Questions for Personal Reflection
or Group Discussion

1. Does praying for business success ever make you feel guilty? If so, why do you think that is?

2. Today we explored three biblical scenarios of praying for work success. Which of these three most resonates with you, and why?
   - Praying for the success of a specific idea (e.g., Nehemiah).
   - Praying for the success of a specific task (e.g., Abraham's servant).
   - Praying for success against a specific threat (e.g., King David).

3. What changes would you like to see in the way you pray about your work, and what is one specific step you might take to implement a change?

PLANNING:

If **GOD** Is Sovereign, Why **PLAN?**

MY FRIEND ROD COOPER, who grew up in a rough situation, quipped that early in his spiritual pilgrimage his life philosophy was, "Trust God . . . and have a great backup plan." We can laugh at that, but simply put, trusting God and planning are not mutually exclusive.

Some, no doubt, will see planning as evidence that we lack faith God will take care of us. They will remember that Jesus told His followers to pray for "daily" bread, and not to worry about tomorrow, "for tomorrow will worry about it-self"(Matthew 6:34). However, the Bible has a lot to say about making plans.

Most Plans Don't Work Out

Unfortunately, the odds are against our plans succeeding. Approximately two-thirds of all new initiatives fail. This appears to be the case without regard to sector, whether for profit, nonprofit, public, private, business, government, education, or health care—and it makes no difference if the idea is a product, a program, a process, or an entire business:

- *Products:* Booz-Allen and Hamilton Inc. found that 86 percent of all new products ideas never make it to market. In the same study, they found 50 percent to 70 percent of the new products that do make it to market—or about two-thirds of all new initiatives—fail.[1] Similarly, MIT's *Sloan Management Review* reports that 70 percent or more of newly launched products fail.[2]
- *Programs:* In existing organizations, a full two-thirds of all new organizational change initiatives fail.[3] Examples include strategic change initiatives, restructurings, customer relationship management (CRM), quality management (e.g., TQM, Six Sigma), cultural makeovers, corporate renewals, reengineering, programs (e.g., training, loss prevention, safety), and technological innovations.
- *Businesses:* The U.S. Bureau of Labor Statistics found that 56 percent of new business start-ups fail within four years.[4] Big companies are not immune. Since 1955, more than 1,800 different companies have appeared on the Fortune 500 list.[5] That means at least 1,300 companies rotated off the list. How does it happen that organizations that grow so big and help so many can fall from grace? Moreover, what are the companies still on the list doing differently?

The cost of failure is steep. When a plan fails to reach sustainability, the unraveled dream can be expensive: damaged (or ruined) careers, missed opportunities, deflated values, and lost time.[6]

So why do some ideas succeed while others languish or fail? Some ideas, of course, just don't want to work. However, many executives and managers have great ideas, but they don't understand what's required to *systematically* turn those ideas into lasting change through good planning.[7] For example, the American Management Association surveyed two thousand companies, and found executives and managers didn't understand how to create a system to bring about innovations, from finding the right idea to successfully implementing it.[8]

How can your plans be in the one-third that succeed?

Simple personal determination is not a wise strategy. The planning tools of your industry are essential, of course, but the Bible says as much about planning as any business topic. What advice does the Bible offer?

God Has a Plan

The first thing we see in the Bible is that God has a sovereign plan—a plan that will always prevail. Consider the Proverbs:

> To man belong the plans of the heart, but from the Lord comes the reply of the tongue. (16:1)

> The Lord works out everything for his own ends—even the wicked for a day of disaster. (16:4)

> In his heart a man plans his course, but the Lord determines his steps. (16:9)

> Many are the plans in a man's heart, but it is the Lord's purpose that prevails. (19:21)

> There is no wisdom, no insight, no plan that can succeed against the Lord. (21:30)

The New Testament also attests the certainty of God's plan prevailing. Jesus said, "Are not two sparrows sold for a penny? Yet not one of them will fall to the ground apart from the will of your Father. . . . So don't be afraid; you are worth more than many sparrows" (Matthew 10:29–31). Even a bird can't fall out of the sky unless it happens according to God's plan.

And then there is Ephesians 1:11, which says, "In him we were also chosen, having been predestined according to the plan of him who works out everything in conformity with the purpose of his will."

But here's a crucial question: If God's plan is going to prevail anyway, and if, on top of that, we are exhorted by Jesus not to worry about tomorrow, why bother with planning?

Actually, it is precisely because God's plans always prevail that making plans that align with His will is worth the effort. Biblically speaking, the two-thirds of ideas that fail do so because they are not part of God's will.

Life is messy, but it is messy according to God's will. In fact, if your life is not a little messy, you are probably not taking enough risks, as the following story about the Olive Garden restaurant chain illustrates.

Making Plans for
Olive Garden Italian Restaurants

Through sports car racing, I've become friends with Brad Blum, chief executive officer of Macaroni Grill—and formerly CEO of Burger King and of Olive Garden Italian Restaurants.

Brad was asked to become the CEO of Olive Garden at a time when same-store sales were sliding fast—12 percent in the year before he took over. So before he agreed to assume the position, Brad wanted to seek advice and assess the situation. As part of his plan he went "undercover," working at several Olive Garden restaurants over a period of seven weeks.

Among other jobs, he served as a kitchen helper. One day he saw a chef stick his bare hand down a filthy drain, pull out a glob of things that shouldn't be there, and throw it away. Then, after only slightly rinsing his hand, without using soap, he stuck the same hand into a drawer, picked up a handful of pasta, and put it into a sauté pan.

In his role as a kitchen helper, Brad said, "You know, I haven't been here that long, and I'm the new guy, but that doesn't seem right. Shouldn't you have washed your hands?" The cook sneered at him with a withering look and kept doing his work. From experiences like these, Brad made a long list of the things he wanted to change.

After seven weeks, Brad accepted the position, saying, "I want Olive Garden to be a fine Italian dining experience."

One of his first tasks was to assemble the senior leadership team, who, unlike him, had never been involved in the actual operations of the restaurants. Instead, they had been content to stay in their offices and read regional reports. He told them as gently as he could, "You cannot continue to behave in this fashion and be so oblivious to the destruction around you. We have to make dramatic changes. We can start with marketing and make a change immediately, but that is only going to help us for a little while. The whole basic culture has to change, our whole focus and operation."

It wasn't easy. The resistance to his plans from some in senior leadership was substantial for the first several years.

But Brad had a plan, and he was determined. He started an Olive Garden restaurant in Italy. He began rotating the chefs in and out of that restaurant, so they could learn to cook the Italian way. He partnered with an Italian winery. He increased training for employees by 500 percent.[9]

Eventually his ideas began to gain traction. From Tuscany, he imported some marble plaques. He engraved the name of the general manager of each restaurant on a plaque. Then he bolted the plaques to the buildings, illuminating them with twenty-four-hour lights. He told each manager, "You are like the president of this restaurant. This is your restaurant. Don't treat this like a chain restaurant. We are here to help you succeed to the very best of your ability."

Almost immediately, the plan succeeded. Olive Garden experienced thirty-three consecutive quarters of growth under Brad's watch. Same store sales almost doubled, and profits rose 600 percent. And good planning played an enormous role.

Brad's experience supports a point Solomon made: "The plans of the diligent lead to profit as surely as haste leads to poverty" (Proverbs 21:5).

Planning is a biblical necessity. Determination without a plan means you can only succeed by accident. Planning, of course, doesn't guarantee success, but failing to plan almost always leads to failure.

> **GOD'S PLANS ALWAYS PREVAIL, SO MAKING PLANS THAT ALIGN WITH HIS WILL IS WORTH THE EFFORT.**

As we saw in the Olive Garden story, the senior management's inattention to the details of their business was a harbinger of bad things to come. Solomon wrote, "Be sure you know the condition of your flocks, give careful attention to your herds; for riches do not endure forever, and a crown is not secure for all generations" (Proverbs 27:23–24).

And, of course, we have to work our plans. "A little sleep, a little slumber, a little folding of the hands to rest—and poverty will come on you like a bandit and scarcity like an armed man" (Proverbs 24:33–34).

Your plan doesn't have to be elaborate. In an executive program I attended at the Harvard Business School, for owners and presidents of smaller companies, I learned that operators of smaller enterprises often don't have written plans. That doesn't mean they don't have plans—just not written plans. Successful people plan, even if they keep it in their heads.[10]

Remember the big idea of this chapter: Because God's plans always prevail, making plans that align with His will is worth the effort.

How to Align with God's Plans

Scripture also gives some specifics about how to plan.

1. *Seek advice.* "Plans fail for lack of counsel, but with many advisers they succeed," Proverbs 15:22 tells us. Get advice from many people whose opinions you respect.

2. *Take time to pray.* Proverbs 21:31 puts planning in the context of a battle, saying, "The horse is made ready for the day of battle, but victory rests with the Lord." God decides what will succeed, so we need to pray and consult Him in the planning process. It should be, "pray, then plan," not "plan, then pray." Don't make plans, and then ask God to bless them. Involve Him in the process of preparing a strategy.

3. *Align with God's plans.* Proverbs 16:3 admonishes, "Commit to the Lord whatever you do, and your plans will succeed." If we bring our plans into alignment with God's plans in the first place, the Bible tells us that our plans will then succeed. Align your plans with God's redemptive purposes. Then, even when implementation becomes messy, you can rest in the understanding that your plans are under the protection of His plans. Everything you want to accomplish hinges on its alignment with God's plan.

4. *Show humility.* James 4:13–16 (mentioned earlier) explains that an assuming or boastful attitude can get us into trouble—but humble submission to God's will brings us into alignment:

Now listen, you who say, "Today or tomorrow we will go to this or that city, spend a year there, carry on business and make money." Why, you do not even know what will happen tomorrow. What is your life? You are a mist that appears for a little while and then vanishes. Instead, you ought to say, "If it is the Lord's will, we will live and do this or that." As it is, you boast and brag. All such boasting is evil.

When Plans Don't Work Out

Because of the fall, whatever plan we pick will bring a lot of hard work. That's why it is so crucial to pick the right strategy and plan, because if you pick the wrong plan, you may not know it for several years, despite lots of hard work.

God's Greater Good

Even when we are in God's will, sometimes the Lord has a greater good that requires our plans to not work out. The apostle Paul made lots of plans—some of them came to fruition, and some didn't. To the Christians in Rome, for instance, Paul wrote, "I do not want you to be unaware, brothers, that I planned many times to come to you (but have been prevented from doing so until now)" (Romans 1:13).

And Luke reported, "Paul and his companions traveled throughout the region of Phrygia and Galatia, having been kept by the Holy Spirit from preaching the word in the province of Asia. When they came to the border of Mysia, they tried to enter Bithynia, but the Spirit of Jesus would not allow them to" (Acts 16:6–7).

That's one of the hazards of planning—it doesn't always work. So how should we respond when our plans don't materialize? Proverbs 20:24 reminds us, "A man's steps are directed by the Lord. How then can anyone understand his own way?" When our plans don't work out, we can rest in the assurance that our plans are under the protection of His plans.

God's Sovereign Plan and a Lakefront Lot

Let me give you an example of a personal business deal. I have always wanted to live on a lake. My wife and I talked about this for years. By the time our son was in the tenth grade, we had pretty much decided we would stay right where we were. We figured we'd wait for two years until he graduated. Then we could move anywhere in the world that we wanted.

One day I was checking rental rates on some commercial properties. I took a shortcut and drove by a sign that said, "Lakefront lot for sale." Instinctively, I veered down the road to see the lot. I hadn't been thinking about acting on this whim, but later I mentioned it to my wife, Patsy, and we decided to look at it together.

Patsy is a deliberate person, so it surprised me when she said, "Let's buy it!"

I said, "I didn't bring you here to work you."

"I know," she replied, "but let's buy it!"

I called the seller, we met that Saturday morning, came to an agreement, and then went home.

About 1:00 p.m. my phone rang. It was the seller. "Pat," he said. "I'm calling because I've known this man for a while, and he asked me to call him if I ever wanted to sell that lot. After I left you, I called him. He wants the lot. I feel duty-bound to you, so if you give me ten thousand dollars more than he will give me, it's yours."

I've been around this block once or twice before, so I said, "I thought this morning we made a deal, a bargain, and we shook on it."

He replied, "Well, yeah, but that was before I called this other guy."

"I don't understand what that has to do with anything," I said.

"It's that he is willing to pay more, but I want you to have it."

We parried back and forth like that a few times. Finally I said, "If it's God's sovereign plan for us to have this lot, then nothing can prevent that from happening. If it is not His plan, then no amount of me begging you will make a difference. So do what you need to do."

There was a long pause—maybe twenty seconds or more, and he said, "Well, okay, since you put it that way you can have the lot." That's where Patsy and I built the house where we now live.

Here is the assurance we can compile from Scripture: No wisdom, no insight, no plan can succeed against the Lord. His will always prevails. Therefore, when we make our plans by seeking advice, prayer, and humbly committing our plans to God, either our plans will succeed, or we can rest in the knowledge that God is sovereignly orchestrating all human events to a good end.

So, why should we bother to plan? Because *any plan in humble alignment with the will of God will succeed.* Our plans are under the protection of His plans.

A PRAYER YOU CAN PRAY

Heavenly Father, thank You that I don't have to plan my life on my own. Like a lieutenant reporting to a general, I receive from You lots of leeway to plan my own battles, yet You still control the master plan. When I have plans that are not working out, help me to remember that I am under Your protection and You will not allow me to destroy myself with some plan. When plans don't work out, it is for good, not for harm. Also, help me to align myself with Your larger purposes. Everything I do hinges on that. No wisdom, no insight, no plan will ever succeed against the Lord. But when I commit my plans to You, they will succeed.

So give me this insight as a long-term way of thinking—a whole new mind-set for the future. I ask this in Jesus' name, amen.

Questions for Personal Reflection
or Group Discussion

1. Do your plans generally work out or not, and why?

2. The Bible emphatically states that God's plans always prevail (see Proverbs 16:9; 19:21; 21:30; and Ephesians 1:11). If God's plan is going to prevail anyway, and if, on top of that, we are exhorted by Jesus not to worry about tomorrow (Matthew 6:34), why bother with planning?

3. What is something you have been planning? What have you read in this chapter that may change or influence your thinking?

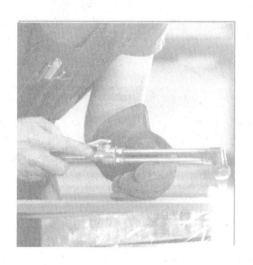

LEADERSHIP:

The CRAFTING of a LEADER

STEVE WAS THE FOUNDER AND CEO of a large, privately held trucking company. To create a professional atmosphere, all the company's executives wore business suits to work. One year Steve returned from vacation with a pair of cowboy boots, which he started wearing to the office.

Within six months, all the executives of the company were also wearing cowboy boots to work.

After a year or so, Steve lost interest in his boots and stopped wearing them. Within a few months all the other executives also returned to their regular shoes.

Everything boils down to leadership.

Leaders are vested with great influence. This influence is out of proportion: therefore it creates sobering responsibility. To whom much is given, much will be required (see Luke 12:48).

You may be a leader by position or not, but everyone has influence over others—whether a supervisor, customer service rep, salesman, or tradesman. You may or may not lead by position, but we all lead by example.

The essence of leadership is the ability to inspire people to get things done, and all that this implies. Leadership is about finding a way to touch the noble impulse within every human being. Whether in management or not, leaders are the indispensable catalysts who ignite great ideas. If the idea is the dynamite, then leadership is the fuse. Just as many nonmanagers can be leaders, many managers are not true leaders. To see the differences between managing and leading, see the chart titled "Leaders Versus Managers," on the next page.

Many writers and experts believe the United States is experiencing a leadership crisis. I happen to agree. Leadership is lacking; it's broken; there simply are not enough strong leaders to go around.

We might be tempted to think the Bible doesn't have much to say about the leadership issues we are confronting. But leadership issues aren't new, only the circumstances. The questions remain the same, regardless of the time in which they are asked. And frankly, to a great extent, the answers remain the same as well.

The Bible describes men who excelled as leaders, even in situations of great difficulty. Moses was one of the most phenomenal leaders mentioned in all of Scripture. He encountered the same problems that any contemporary leader will face. Let's explore how his leadership principles apply to today's work world.

How and Why God Crafts a Leader

In the first-century church, Stephen was tried on charges of blasphemy. In a gripping defense, he described how the Hebrew people ended up in slavery in Egypt. He said, "As the time drew near for God to fulfill his promise to Abraham, the number of our people in Egypt greatly increased. Then another king, who knew nothing about Joseph, became ruler of Egypt. He dealt treacherously with our people and oppressed our forefathers by forcing them to throw out their newborn babies so that they would die" (Acts 7:17–19).

Moses, Scene 1: Development

It's impossible to imagine live babies being tossed into a river to drown, but that's exactly what was happening. Against that backdrop Moses was born. And "he was no ordinary child," Stephen reminded his audience (Acts 7:20).

Leaders Versus Managers[1]

Leaders	Managers
Push for change	Maintain an even keel
Think about ideas	Think about planning and execution
Cast the vision	Chart the course
Shape the future	Oversee the existing order
Are visionary and strategic	Are strategic and operational
Incite people to see what could be	Focus on accomplishing existing goals
Enlist people to the cause	Mobilize people through structure
Move people to action	Direct people to accomplish goals
Seek risk	Seek control
Shake things up	Smooth things out
Live with ambiguity	Seek stability
Delay closure	Act to solve problems quickly
Look for big gains at big risk	Look for compromises so everyone wins
Focus on substance of an issue	Focus on following the correct procedures
Send "messages"	Send "signals"

Moses was only three months old when his mother placed him in a basket in the river to avoid possible death. Eventually Pharaoh's daughter discovered the floating basket and soon adopted Moses as her own son (Exodus 2:1–10). Stephen recalled, "Moses was educated in all the wisdom of the Egyptians and was powerful in speech and action" (Acts 7:22).

That ends scene one. And it gives a powerful suggestion for developing yourself as a leader. The prequel to the story of your leadership is a good education, because it will help make you powerful in speech and action—confident and prepared to lead. And, personally, I've also found it valuable to my own leadership to be a lifelong learner.

Moses, Scene 2: Rejection

Now let's move on to scene two. When Moses was forty years old, he visited the Hebrew people. Moses saw an Egyptian mistreating a Hebrew slave, came to his defense, and killed the Egyptian. "Moses thought that his own people would realize that God was using him to rescue them, but they did not" (Acts 7:25). The next day, Moses tried to reconcile two Israelites who were fighting, and one of them said, "Who made you ruler and judge over us? Do you want to kill me as you killed the Egyptian yesterday?" (Acts 7:27–28).

Hearing that, Moses fled to the wilderness, where he settled as a foreigner, married, and had two sons. So even though Moses was a capable leader—educated, credentialed, powerful in speech and action—his leadership was rejected. He thought God had called him to deliver his people from bondage. He thought he was adequately prepared. But when he tried to execute the vision, his people rejected him.

So in his first forty years, Moses thought he had developed to the point that his leadership was adequate. As it turned out, he was wrong. He was judged inadequate, despite his personal attributes and his preparation. Perhaps there was too much Moses in Moses. Throughout Scripture we find that, as He deals with leaders, God is always more interested in the success of character than in the success of circumstances. He never sacrifices character to improve circumstances, but he will sacrifice our circumstances to build character.

Moses, Scene 3: Isolation and Equipping

For the next forty years, Moses wandered the wilderness tending sheep in apparent failure and isolation. God wanted to remove some things from Moses' character, and He wanted to build some things into his character.

Moses' wilderness experience was like a smelting pot. To make steel, you start with iron. But you have to apply extremely high heat to remove the "slag"—the impurities that bubble to the top and can be removed—so only the steel remains. The big idea for this chapter is that *hot fire makes good character*. God equips us to lead by taking us through trials—and sometimes failures—that strengthen us to serve others, whether at work or home.

Moses was strong and powerful in his speech and action. He was a tough guy.

He was hard. He was educated. But he relied on his own best thinking. He had a God-shaped vision to deliver his people, but he tried to execute before God called him to execute. But out in the wilderness, God forged Moses into the kind of leader who could respond to such a big calling. He does the same for us—He is more interested in our long-term character development than our immediate success.

Moses, Scene 4: Calling and Sending

"After forty years had passed, an angel appeared to Moses" (Acts 7:30). You know the story. Moses saw a bush that appeared to be on fire, but it was not consumed by the flame. Moses stopped to investigate. Then God spoke and said, "I have indeed seen the oppression of my people in Egypt. I have heard their groaning and have come down to set them free. Now come, I will send you back to Egypt" (Acts 7:34).

At this point, Moses was eighty years old, and now God was sending him back to the place where he had failed. But now we find a much different Moses. His early confidence had given way to doubt. That's what forty years of humbling will do! Moses basically said, "God, I can't do this! Please send someone else" (see Exodus 3:11–4:13). Forty years of replaying what could have been had melted his personal confidence. He had lost sight of the vision. He was dispirited and couldn't figure out why God would bother with him after all those years.

Stephen explained the situation like this: "This is the same Moses whom they had rejected with the words, 'Who made you ruler and judge?' He was sent to be their ruler and deliverer by God himself, through the angel who appeared to him in the bush. He led them out of Egypt and did wonders and miraculous signs in Egypt, at the Red Sea, and for forty years in the desert" (Acts 7:35–36).

IF YOU ARE IN THE SMELTING POT, GOD IS NOT TRYING TO BREAK YOU; HE IS TRYING TO MAKE YOU.

Isn't it interesting? What we often view as abandonment is equipping us. God sent Moses into the wilderness for forty years to equip him to lead his people. Sure, Moses felt abandoned. We all have felt abandoned. But God is always focused on the main thing, to sovereignly orchestrate all of the seemingly random circumstances of our lives—and leadership—to bring people into right relationship with Him and right relationship with each other. Imagine for a moment how catastrophic it would have been for Moses to deliver his people from slavery into a wilderness of which he knew nothing—for forty years!

Whatever you are going through as a leader, God is using your circumstances to equip you to lead in a greater way at a future time. Again, hot fire makes good character. If you are in the smelting pot, God is not trying to break you; He is trying to make you.

Implications for Your Leadership

From Moses' story, here are three implications for leadership today:

1. Listen to the Words, "You Are a Leader"

The first step in becoming a leader is to have someone tell you, "You're a leader." I was well into my forties and had always been leading—in high school, in the army, in college, in business, ministry, family, and community. I've always been given leadership responsibility. But when someone would say, "I really would appreciate your leadership on this," I always felt uncomfortable. That's because no "elder" or mentor had ever blessed me and said, "You're a leader."

It took me twenty-five years of adult life—well into my forties—to realize I am a leader. But once I believed it, that knowledge turned my life upside down. It has been so liberating, so freeing to know that I'm a leader.

Moses was brought up to think he was a leader. And then, when he doubted it in the wilderness, God affirmed his leadership by saying, in essence, "You're a leader." If no one has told you that you are a leader, may I do that for you right now? You're a leader, you can do it, and you can make a difference.

2. Be Careful as You Evaluate the Data

It is easy to look at the data and come to the wrong conclusion. Moses looked at the data—the mistreatment of his people—and came to the wrong conclusion: "It's time to act on my vision to deliver these people from slavery." Instead, God told Moses to wait, and He sent the would-be leader into exile.

Coming to the wrong or premature conclusion can happen to any of us. I remember putting together a real estate development project. I studied data that indicated exactly what my company needed at the time. We needed cash flow. All the numbers worked on paper, but I wasn't really listening to God. I wanted to put this deal together, so I appealed to my own determination rather than seek any leadership from the Holy Spirit. I really believed this was the only way to solve the problem, so I tried to force the deal to happen.

But the lender refused to give me the construction financing, so I flew to the city where they were located. One of my greatest strengths is that I can be pretty persuasive, and one of my greatest weaknesses is that I can be pretty persuasive. In the flesh, I made the best case ever for a construction loan on a development deal! Yes, I got that deal done, but it is easy to look at the data and come to the wrong conclusion.

So we built a business park—and then no one rented the space.

If you find yourself trying to force your leadership to work, reconsider your options. Perhaps you've been properly educated and credentialed, perhaps you even come from the right "family." You may be completely capable and adequate and persuasive. Even with all those things going for you, you can still look at the data and come to the wrong conclusion. You can force the deal if you want to, but in the long term, you may be sorry.

3. God Is Most Interested in Your Character

Remember that God is more interested in character success than circumstance success.

In his excellent book *The Making of a Leader*, Robert Clinton describes a "plateau leader," which he calls the most common category of leader. Clinton's research shows that leaders who plateau early reveal a common pattern. They learn new skills until they can operate comfortably. But once they achieve those skills, the leaders deliberately fail to seek new skills, and they habitually coast on prior experience.

There are two errors for us to avoid in our leadership. First is forcing our leadership, as with Moses. Second is slacking off in our leadership and coast. To do either is to fail.

Who doesn't want to build a comfortable world and then coast? When we are in the smelting pot, we tend to want to get out and build a comfortable world and just coast. If we truly want to be all God wants us to be, we must accept the smelting pot as part of our refining. If we want to be powerful and more effective in leadership, we have to remember that hot fire makes good steel—and character.

Being a great leader means being ready to sacrifice, demonstrating integrity, and being persistent, among other qualities. To understand what makes a great leader, see "Visionaries" below.

Visionaries
What Great Leaders Are Like and How to Be One

What makes a great leader? Every now and then a leader is called to a task so big that few can equal the challenge. Above all else, these leaders are visionary. And because of them, the world spins a little more smoothly. What makes these leaders tick?

Here are eleven traits of great leaders. Together, they spell *visionaries*. Notice that several of these traits, including sacrifice, integrity, and perseverance, are character qualities.

- *Vision.* More than anything else, great leaders are propelled by great dreams. They're pulled along by the grip of destiny. Invariably, the force of their personalities pulls us along with them.
- *Innovation.* Great leaders give the world "ideas" that change the existing order. They exude creativity and imagination. They embrace an uncertain future.
- *Sacrifice.* Great leaders deny themselves for a greater good. They're so committed to their cause that they are willing to risk rejection.
- *Integrity.* At their core, great leaders have unwavering character. A handshake still means everything to them. This inspires confidence.
- *Optimism.* Great leaders possess a passion that touches that noble impulse in each of us. They inspire us to want to be part of something bigger than ourselves.

- *Never giving up.* Great leaders display unwavering belief in their mission. Against all odds they show tenacity, perseverance, and faithfulness to their call. Their motivation rests on deeply held principles, not opinion polls.
- *Ability.* Great leaders possess special abilities. They are people of skill, whether inventor, philosopher, theologian, scientist, artist, writer, poet, or preacher. They possess innate intelligence.
- *Relate to others.* Great leaders have empathy and love for people. Their people skills include compassion and listening. They relate to people from all walks of life.
- *Improbability.* Great leaders never think they are great. They are marked by a profound humility. The world would not pick them. And if in their own lifetimes they become great, they are the last ones to know.
- *Excellence.* Great leaders demand excellence from themselves, which spurs us to be like them. Their striving for excellence is often confused with perfectionism.
- *Servant of others.* Great leaders are first servants. They exist to leave the world a better place by loving and serving others.

Real-World Situations

Now let's apply these ideas to real-world situations.

1. You've Come to the Wrong Conclusion

You're a capable leader. You get things done. But you looked at the data and came to the wrong conclusion. Now what do you do?

When Moses thought he was adequate for the vision of leading, God found him inadequate. Then when Moses found himself inadequate, God found him adequate. *God can use an inadequate man who will acknowledge that he is inadequate.*

Maybe you are capable, and now the message is to remember that hot fire makes good steel. When you get burned, humble yourself before the Holy God.

I'll tell you what happened on the deal I mentioned earlier, where I forced a project on wrong conclusions. One day I drove to Vero Beach, Florida, to speak at a prayer breakfast. On the way back, I got off the interstate and drove around in the empty business park. When I looked at all the empty buildings that no one was leasing, I remember being so distraught.

I drove behind the buildings, found a patch of grass, got out of my car, laid prostrate on the ground, and begged God to give me relief. I asked Him to do whatever was necessary to perfect my character. "Lord, this is so painful," I said. "But I do know this—I want to be a leader, and I give You permission to do what You must, to craft me into the leader You want me to be. If failure here is what it takes for me to be usable, then You go ahead and do it." And He did. But the character development that resulted was priceless.

2. You Feel Dispirited and Discouraged

Perhaps you've been in the wilderness a long time. How should you react when you are dispirited and discouraged? I urge you, don't pray for God to reduce the duration of your hard times. Instead, ask Him to give you grace and to help you learn everything He has for you during this hard time. Learn. Let the hot fire make you into good steel, refining your character and faith in Him.

3. You Are a Young Leader and Feel Unprepared

If you're a younger leader, you are at the beginning of this process. How can you make your life count the way that you really dream about? First, regardless of circumstances, remember you are a leader. Second, declare yourself before a watching world.

Nineteenth-century American evangelist Dwight Moody went to England when he was a young man. He heard someone say, "It remains to be seen what God will do with a man who gives himself up wholly unto him." Moody responded, "I will be that man." He didn't say he would be a great man or a rich man. He just said he would be a consecrated man—he declared himself. And God used Moody mightily to bring revival in his work in the United States and abroad.

The prophet Jeremiah declared himself. He was in stocks, in prison for proclaiming the truth of God's Word. And when he was released, he basically said,

"Lord, I don't understand. I do all this work for You, and instead of getting a reward, I am mobbed and insulted." Then he turned his attention to his own journal, and he wrote, "But if I say, 'I will not mention him or speak any more in his name,' his word is in my heart like a fire, a fire shut up in my bones. I am weary of holding it in; indeed, I cannot" (Jeremiah 20:9).

Declare yourself. You will be God's leader. You can be good steel, if you will accept the fire and let God mold you.

A PRAYER YOU CAN PRAY

Lord Jesus, thank You for the example of Moses, who showed how we can become more powerful and effective in our leadership. I pray that when I look at facts in order to make decisions, I would not come to the wrong conclusions. For those times I do, help me to humble myself and repent and not ask for a shortened duration, but for character success. When I become discouraged, I pray that You would encourage me in the wilderness. Remind me that there is an end to this, and that You will use me in a greater way because of this wilderness experience. Finally, help me to declare myself as sold out for You.

Take all Christian leadership—mine and that of other followers of Jesus—out into the marketplace, so Your kingdom would expand through our humble direction. I ask this in Jesus' name, amen.

Questions for Personal Reflection
or Group Discussion

1. How did God craft Moses' life and leadership? How does this compare to how God has crafted your own life and leadership?

2. Pick one of the following statements and explain how it can apply to your leadership:
   - Determination, in and of itself, is not a strategy.
   - There was too much Moses in Moses.
   - God is more interested in the success of our character than the success of our circumstances.
   - God can use an inadequate man who will acknowledge his inadequacy.

3. Did anyone ever tell you, "You're a leader"? How has that impacted your life?

CHAPTER

FAILURES:

How to Handle **FAILURE**

WHEN TOM WATSON WAS CHIEF executive officer of IBM, he put a young executive in charge of a major project. The junior executive promptly lost ten million dollars. Watson summoned the young man to his office. The executive said, "I guess you're looking for my resignation."

Watson replied, "You've got to be kidding! We just invested ten million dollars in your education. You're not going anywhere!"[1]

Everyone fails from time to time. As noted in chapter 10, about two-thirds of all new initiatives fail. Because of the fall and how God uses the fall to help sovereignly orchestrate human events, failure is inevitable.

For recreation, my wife loves human drama. She reads books about broken lives and watches movies about people facing difficulties. She finds it exhilarating.

I am not motivated that way. I have enough of "real life" in my work. I don't want to spend my leisure time dealing with other people's thorny issues. I go to the movies to be entertained, to escape and have fun—to get some relief from marketplace reality. I am well aware that life is hard, in both personal and professional settings.

In fact, in the professional setting, life is so hard that "marketplace reality" is often a pseudonym for failure. Business collapses come in many shapes and sizes, and they have many causes.

- New products don't catch on with the public.
- New programs or initiatives don't live up to their billing.
- Cheaper competition compels companies to downsize.
- Recessions force organizations to do layoffs.

Failure is part of the fabric of business. In fact, most of us with a lengthy business history would agree that it's unavoidable.

Four Reasons Business Ideas Fail

Businesses and careers can derail—even fail—because of poor judgment, poor execution, external factors beyond our control, or sin.

In the movie *The Pursuit of Happyness*, Chris Gardner (Will Smith) invests his life savings in a set of diagnostic machines that scan bone density. Unfortunately, the margin of improvement, when compared to the price, renders the purchase impractical. He works hard—but he can't sell the machines. His failure is based on *an error in judgment*. That's one of the most frequently cited reasons for business failure.

A second cause may be *poor execution*. During a previous book project, I met with the publisher's team to determine a marketing plan. A year passed, and we had a follow-up meeting. They said, "Let's talk about the future." I said, "First let's talk about the last twelve months. I want to go through each item of agreement from our meeting a year ago, and I want to get a status report. I want accountability on that."

So we went through the list, but they had not completed even one item from the previous year's plan. Then they said, in essence, that even though they had failed to execute the plan, I should lower my expectations. I said, "No, I don't think this is going to work out." That failure was caused by poor execution.

And then, sometimes, failures result from *external reasons* over which we have no control—like an economic meltdown. Perhaps a competitor releases a better product. Maybe a business partner makes poor choices that affect everyone around him.

And finally, sometimes it's sin. Pride influences our decisions. We refuse to acknowledge that we made a mistake, so rather than correcting it, we make it worse. Or we make an idol out of something and pursue it, despite the cost.

The Personal Toll of Failure

Regardless of the cause, business failure is devastating. The personal collateral damage is staggering. You have no doubt seen, and I know I have seen, people endure extreme hardships, including divorce, bankruptcy, loss of confidence, loss of reputation, suicide, alcoholism, and substance abuse. Often, the failure of one person affects a lot of innocent people—innocent in the sense that they had no part in a particular failure. Yet, those innocent people still suffer— like the downtown businesses in the small Minnesota town I mentioned in the chapter on prayer.

Bill's business went under because of mismanagement. Hundreds of employees lost their jobs. Bill lost his family in a divorce. When I met him he was living out of his office. He was depressed, disheveled, and slovenly. His office looked like a tornado had swept through it. It was pathetic. In the middle of the chaos, however, was a photo on a credenza that had been carefully placed and safeguarded—a picture of a sailboat with a little girl. I asked who she was, and for the first time, Bill's voice showed signs of life. He explained that she was his daughter, and how she was the only reason he had left for living.

I asked, "What's her name?"

"Jennifer," he said with such deep affection that I was moved. So much so, in fact, that when my wife, Patsy, and I had our first child, we named her Jennifer.

Because of what twentieth-century Christian philosopher Francis Schaeffer called "the domino effect of the fall," we must all manage the effects of the sin. We have to manage our lives against the fall.

Making It Personal

So how are you doing? Have you stumbled? Maybe you erred in judgment. Maybe you sinned with a moral indiscretion. Or maybe you got sideswiped by the competition and the general realities of the marketplace. Unfortunately, Christianity is not an inoculation against the domino effect of the fall. We are not immune to failure. We all still sin and fall short. When an investment tanks, we lose money at the same rate as the nonbeliever. What a Christian in business does have, however, is a God who is profoundly interested in walking through your failures as a father with his son. We have private access to the King of Kings who, even though He doesn't grant immunity from failure, does promise to give us wisdom and power to navigate through our failures.

So in the face of failure, is there any advantage to being a Christian? Yes. The big idea for this chapter is this: *If I am a Christian, I can manage against the fall as a son of God, and not as an orphan.* The nonbeliever faces the disadvantage of experiencing failure without appeal to the most-high God.

Managing Failure as a Son

Hebrews 12 gives excellent advice to manage failure as a son of God. The first thing we see is Jesus' example. He is our Lord, Savior, and leader, but He also is our big brother. He provides the example of son-like behavior.

> Therefore, since we are surrounded by such a great cloud of witnesses, let us throw off everything that hinders and the sin that so easily entangles, and let us run with perseverance the race marked out for us. Let us fix our eyes on Jesus, the author and perfecter of our faith, who for the joy set before him endured the cross, scorning its shame, and sat down at the right hand of the throne of God. Consider him who endured such opposition from sinful men, so that you will not grow weary and lose heart. In your struggle against sin, you have not yet resisted to the point of shedding your blood. (Hebrews 12:1–4)

"Let us fix our eyes on Jesus." Do that, and we won't grow weary and lose heart. The non-Christian is at a tremendous disadvantage. Where does he look for encouragement? The world tells him, "Just suck it up, buddy, and keep going." He's on his own. But as believers, we have opportunity to consider how Jesus endured opposition from sinful men. We look to Him as our example, and He sustains us.

Let's pick up the Scripture passage again:

And you have forgotten that word of encouragement that addresses you as sons: 'My son, do not make light of the Lord's discipline, and do not lose heart when he rebukes you, because the Lord disciplines those he loves, and he punishes everyone he accepts as a son.' Endure hardship as discipline; God is treating you as sons. For what son is not disciplined by his father? If you are not disciplined (and everyone undergoes discipline), then you are illegitimate children and not true sons. (Hebrews 12:5–8)

Most of us had human fathers who disciplined us, and we respected them for it. How much more should we submit to our heavenly Father's discipline? God often uses hardship to discipline us for our good. His intention is that we will share in His holiness. Verse 11 goes on to say, "No discipline seems pleasant at the time, but painful. Later on, however, it produces a harvest of righteousness and peace for those who have been trained by it."

I challenge you to look at your failures as discipline. God might spank you, but He will never beat you. No one ever has to call Child Protective Services because of God's discipline. God will not abuse you.

If you had good parents, or if you are a good parent, you will understand this. A child might stumble, but the parent will be right there. The dad will sacrifice himself so the child doesn't fall. That is what God does in this father-son relationship. No matter how much you stumble, He always will do whatever it takes to restore you. And if you do the grown-up equivalent of skinning your knee, He will minister until you are restored to full health.

I remember when my son John and my daughter Jen were each about a year old. As a rule, moms try to keep things calm, and dads try to stir things up. I was no exception to the rule. I used to throw my kids as high as I could and still keep them safe. I'd toss them two or three feet above my head. They'd squeal with delight, while mom would squeal with terror. She was afraid I would miss catching my child. But you know what? I never missed. I delighted in my children's confident laughter, and I delighted in protecting them from falling. That same principle is active in our relationship with our heavenly Father.

Failure Builds Faith

The last point from that passage in Hebrews 12 is that God uses our failures to build our faith. When circumstances crash down around us, God is not interested in merely restoring the situation. He wants to develop our character. God sees such moments as opportunities to build our faith.

I have to admit—I don't like that. When I am feeling down, discouraged because of failure, I don't care so much about my character. I just want to feel good again. But it's a simple reality—God will never sacrifice our character just to improve our circumstances. Whatever kind of failure you are facing, God is more interested in the success of your character than the success of your circumstances.

That's not to say He's not interested in your circumstances, because He is. But He will not improve your circumstances at the expense of your character. God uses these failures as opportunities to build our faith. We see that clearly revealed in Hebrews 12.

> See to it that you do not refuse him who speaks. If they did not escape when they refused him who warned them on earth, how much less will we, if we turn away from him who warns us from heaven? At that time his voice shook the earth, but now he has promised, "Once more I will shake not only the earth but also the heavens." The words "once more" indicate the removing of what can be shaken—that is, created things—so that what cannot be shaken may remain. Therefore, since we are receiving a kingdom that cannot be shaken, let us be thankful, and so worship God acceptably with reverence and awe, for our "God is a consuming fire." (vv. 25–29)

God is more interested in building your faith than in increasing your things. Clearly, from the text and from our experience, we must manage against the fall.

But we have the advantage over unbelievers, because we manage as sons, not as orphans.

Scriptural Guides to Handling Failure

In light of our "sonship," let's look at some biblical passages that give practical advice for handling failure and disappointment.

1. *Failure is not always punishment.* As we already noted in Hebrews 12, verse 5 tells us, "Do not make light of the Lord's discipline, and do not lose heart when he rebukes you." Keep in mind, discipline is not always punishment for wrongdoing. Sometimes it is preparation for greater service. A marathon competitor disciplines himself to run long distances. If he didn't prepare, he would fail. Sometimes discipline involves small failures, but it prepares us so we don't fail in something more crucial that occurs later. Keep in mind that His discipline is not an expression of His anger, but rather, it demonstrates His loving care.

2. *God will protect you during sudden disaster.* Proverbs 3:25–26 says, "Have no fear of sudden disaster or of the ruin that overtakes the wicked, for the Lord will be your confidence and will keep your foot from being snared." Sometimes you read a verse and it changes your life. That happened the day I found this passage. It reframed a real-estate business failure so I could handle it without growing weary and losing heart.

3. *God will meet your daily needs.* In another time of failure, I found Psalm 37:25: "I was young and now I am old, yet I have never seen the righteous forsaken or their children begging bread." That verse also changed my life when I was at a point where I didn't know if we had enough money to eat. One of the principles of sonship is that we feast on God's Word—and then He opens a door. Use the Scriptures to build your faith. Trust God to give you something that exactly fits your situation.

4. *Don't try to shortcut what God wants to do in your life.* Hebrews 12:7 tells us, "Endure hardship as discipline." Endure it. When you're going through the hard time, don't look for shortcuts. Don't try to shorten the duration of the difficulty, or you may short-circuit what God wants to accomplish

in your life. If you do, you will probably have to travel the same road again.

When my son, John, was in Little League, his team had a time during the season when they won every game. Everyone was so excited. I remember saying to Patsy one day, "You know, winning is building their self-esteem, but they really need to lose a few too, so they can build character." And, of course, eventually it happened—their winning streak snapped. John and his teammates had to manage against the fall, because that's the venue within which they were playing baseball. God uses these things to strike a balance. We need to endure it.

> *FAILURE IS UNAVOIDABLE, BUT WE CAN CHOOSE HOW WE WILL HANDLE IT.*

We submit to the Father because we are sons. As believers, when we get sideswiped, we understand that suffering is part of the sovereignty of a good and loving Father. That same God is able to turn temporal failure into a stepping-stone to eternal success. We don't understand how He does that, but we believe it, we accept it, and we submit to it.

Our Father God has a plan. Sometimes He rewards faithful service by giving you bigger responsibility. Basically, He gives you more chores to do. Sometimes He enjoys tossing you in the air, making you squeal with inexpressible joy. There would be great risk in that if He weren't there to catch you. But He is there, delighting in your delight. And He disciplines, not because He is angry, but because He is nurturing us to maturity. As we trust and endure, He makes it possible for us to manage against the fall, to deal with failure as sons rather than orphans. Failure is unavoidable, but we can choose how we will handle it.

A PRAYER YOU CAN PRAY

Lord Jesus, I fix my eyes on You. Grant me the grace I need to find contentment, peace, and joy in Your will. When I stumble—through error in judgment or sin or for whatever reason—I thank You that You have promised to treat me as Your much-loved son. So I will manage failure as a son, not an orphan.

Build my faith. Give me understanding. Guide me with Your wisdom. I pray this in the mighty name of Jesus, amen.

Questions for Personal Reflection or Group Discussion

1. What's the last work failure you had to face, and how did you get through it?

2. Hebrews 12 gives a number of exhortations that can be applied to handling work failures. Of the four below, which one resonates with you most, and why?
   - 12:5a _____
   - 12:5b _____
   - 12:7 _____
   - 12:9 _____

3. What have you read in the sections of this final chapter shown below that can help you think about and handle failures in a more Christlike way?
   - "Four Reasons Business Ideas Fail"
   - "The Personal Toll of Failure"
   - "Making It Personal"
   - "Managing Failure as a Son"
   - "Failure Builds Faith"
   - "Scriptural Guides to Handling Failure"

Afterword

THE PURPOSE OF THIS BOOK is to help you build a more complete theology of work—a biblical framework to help you think correctly about work and the dozens of subjects we have covered together.

I promised that I would show you how to experience the power of God in your work. I promised you would learn how to bring about social transformation through your work. And I promised to show you how to make your work life count for the glory of God.

I hope you found your investment of time was a good bargain. As you now turn back to your work, my hope and prayer is that you will see it from a fresh, biblical perspective.

Let me close by reminding you of the truth that opened chapter 1: We are an occupation force "ordained" to serve in the markets of men. Remember and accept that your work is not just a platform for ministry—it *is* ministry. We are liberators sent to free a world that labors under "the groan."

We are stewards put in charge until Jesus comes back, and a fifth column called to infiltrate a world stained by sin. We are salt that preserves the way of Christ, and light that leads broken people out of darkness. We are wheat who endure alongside weeds the enemy has sown. We are chameleons who adapt to our culture while never compromising the gospel.

We are ambassadors sent "into" the world that we are at the same time not part "of," taking risks to build Christ's kingdom while not neglecting to tend earth's culture.

We must each do our part as God sovereignly orchestrates "the main thing"— to bring people into right relationship with Him and right relationship with each other. And that is how we will feel most happy, most alive, and most useful.

Notes

Introduction

1. Summary of February 2007 Conference Board report, at http://www.unbossed. com/index.php?itemid=1350.

2. Ralph Mattson and Arthur Miller, *Finding a Job You Can Love* (Nashville: Nelson, 1982), 123.

Chapter 1: Businessman, Plumber, or Minister—Same Thing

1. Francis A. Schaeffer, *Letters of Francis A. Schaeffer* (Westchester, Ill.: Crossway, 1985), 144.

2. Os Guinness, *The Call* (Nashville: Word, 1998), 34–35.

3. Schaeffer, *Letters of Francis A. Schaeffer*, 168.

4. Michael Novak, *Business as a Calling* (New York: Free Press, 1996), 26.

5. Viktor E. Frankl, *Man's Search for Meaning* (New York: Simon and Schuster: 1984), 105.

6. Ibid., 107.

Chapter 2: Why Do We Work?

1. Doug Sherman and William Hendricks, *Your Work Matters to God* (Colorado Springs: NavPress, 1990), 88–89.

2. Ibid., 89.

Chapter 3: The Ten Commandments and the Golden Rule

1. Ronald Reagan, "Address to the National Religious Broadcasters Convention, 30 January 1984, Sheraton Washington Hotel, Washington, D.C.: accessed at http:// www.americanrhetoric.com/speeches/ronaldreagannrbroadcasters.htm.

2. Steve Reinemund, telephone interview, June 2007.

3. Skip Ast, telephone interview, September 2007.

Chapter 4: What Is Our Duty on the Job?

1. Ivy Lee, at http://en.wikipedia.org/wiki/Ivy_Lee.

Chapter 5: Neighbor-Love at Work

1. Peter Drucker, as quoted in George Gilder, *Men and Marriage* (Gretna, La.: Pelican, 1986), 139.

Chapter 6: Authentic Ways to Share Your Faith

1. Dan Cathy, telephone interview, September 2007.

2. Ibid.

3. Ibid.

4. Laura Nash explores the tensions and opportunities that businessmen face about witnessing, from the global public company to the small private organization, in the chapter "Faithful Witness," in Laura Nash, *Believers in Business* (Nashville: Nelson, 1994).

Chapter 7: Promises, Pleasures, and Perils

1. Michael Novak, *Business as a Calling* (New York: The Free Press, 1996), 58ff.

Chapter 8: Temporal Work as a Kingdom Priority

1. Jeff McWaters, telephone interview, March 22, 2007.

2. Jack Alexander, telephone interview, March 26, 2007.

3. Skip Ast, telephone interview, September 2007.

4. Bill Walton, Man in the Mirror Bible study, Orlando, 1998.

Chapter 9: Is It Okay to Pray for Success?

1. Norm Miller, telephone interview, December 2006.

2. Ibid.

Chapter 10: If God Is Sovereign, Why Plan?

1. Booz-Allen and Hamilton, Inc. *New Products Management for the 1980s.* This New York consulting firm published their finding in 1982; obtained from secondary sources.

2. S. Ogawa and F. Piller, "Reducing the Risks of New Product Development," *MIT Sloan Management Review*, 47, no. 2 (Winter 2006): 65.

3. Arthur D. Little and McKinsey & Co. studies cited in Peter M. Senge, Art Kleiner, Charlotte Roberts, and George Roth, *The Dance of Change* (New York: Doubleday, 1999, 5; E. M. Rogers, *Diffusion of Innovations*, 4th ed. (New York: The Free Press, 1995), 371; business intelligence study cited in D. Miller, "Successful Change Leaders," *Journal of Change Management* 2, no. 4 (2002): 360; Gartner Group study cited in Miller (2002); A. Raps, "Implementing Strategy," *Strategic Finance*, 85, no. 12 (2004): 49–53. This appears to be the case without regard to sector, whether public, private, for profit, nonprofit, business, government, education, or health care, e.g., P. Strebel, "Why Do Employees Resist Change?" *Harvard Business Review*, 74, no. 3 (2000): 86–92; P. Pluye, L. Potvin, and J. Denis, "Making Public Health Programs Last: Conceptualizing Sustainability," *Evaluation & Program Planning*, 27, no. 2 (2004): 121–33; R. Yin, *Changing Urban Bureaucracies* (Santa Monica, Calif.: Rand Corporation, 1978).

4. Amy Knaup. "Survival and Longevity in the Business Employment Dynamics Data," *Monthly Labor Review,* May 2005, U.S. Bureau of Labor Statistics, www.bls.gov/opub/mlr/2005/05/ressum.pdf. Accessed March 28, 2007. Similar results were found across all sectors.

5. CNNMoney.com reports that "since 1955, more than 1,800 companies have appeared on the Fortune 500. Many of these companies have changed names over this period, owing to mergers, acquisitions, and bankruptcies. Other companies have gone private or simply changed their names"; www.money.cnn.com/magazines/fortune/fortune500_archive/full/1955/index.html.

6. R. Yin, (1978). *Changing Urban Bureaucracies* (Santa Monica, Calif.: The Rand Corporation 1978).

7. F. Okumus, "A Framework to Implement Strategies in Organizations," *Management Decision,* 41, no. 9 (2003): 871–82.

8. Elizabeth Haas Edersheim, *The Definitive Drucker* (New York: McGraw-Hill, 2007), 103.

9. Brad Blum, telephone interview, January 2007.

10. Philip Thurston, "Should Smaller Companies Make Formal Plans?" *Harvard Business Review,* September–October 1983.

Chapter 11: The Crafting of a Leader

1. Adapted from J. P. Kotter, "What Leaders Really Do," *Harvard Business Review,* 79, no. 11 (1990, repr. 2001): 85–96. A. Zaleznik, "Managers and Leaders: Are They Different?" *Harvard Business Review,* 82, no. 1 (1977, repr. 2004): 74–81.

Chapter 12: How to Handle Failure

1. David A. Garvin, "Building a Learning Organization," *Harvard Business Review,* 71, no. 4 (July/August 1993): 78.

Acknowledgments

AS WITH MOST BOOKS, this one stands on the shoulders of men and women who have made substantial investments into both the author and the manuscript. Thanks to my wife, Patsy, for her constant encouragement. Because of the extraordinary capacities of Daphne Keys, my executive assistant, I was able to focus on this work without distraction. Ruth Ford receives a word of appreciation for converting "Doing Business God's Way"—a series I taught at the Man in the Mirror Bible study—from the spoken to written format. That series became the starting point for this work.

I am also deeply grateful to the entire staff at Man in the Mirror, who so graciously carry on the mission that allows me to withdraw to quiet places where I can write. You are gifts from God: Pam Adkins, Jim Angelakos, Lucy Blair, Ruth Cameron, Sharon Carey, Bernie Clark, Brett Clemmer, David Delk, Tom Hingle, Joanne Hunt, Vanessa Jones, Donna Keiderling, Kelly Laughridge, Al Lenio, Stephanie Lopez, Michael Maine, Dennis Puleo, Scott Russell, Tracie Searles, Jim Seibert, Jamie Smith, Antonio Stevens, and Greg Wilkinson.

So many men allowed me to interview them at length, and I have worked their ideas and, in some cases, their words into the manuscript: Skip Ast, Bob Buford, Brad Blum, Dan Cathy, Bill Heavener, Wayne Huizenga, Jr., Kim Lopdrup, Norm Miller, Steve Reinemund, and Dick Snyder. Thank you.

In addition, I am honored to work with a wonderful team at Moody Publishers—Janis Backing, Dave DeWit, John Hinkley, Steve Lyon, Pam Pugh, Paul Santhouse, Tracey Shannon, Greg Thornton, Jim Vincent, and Keith Wiederwax.

Extra special thanks to Robert Wolgemuth, Erik Wolgemuth, and Andrew Wolgemuth for representing my literary career with such excellence and personal concern.

And what would this book be were it not for the men at the Man in the Mirror Bible study—150 to 200 working men who come together each week to study God's Word and invite Him to transform their lives and unleash them to transform the world?

Additional Resources on the Internet

www.icwm.net

The International Coalition of Workplace Ministries website is a gathering place for workplace ministries. You can view a free directory of many of the best workplace ministries worldwide. Businessmen can find faith-based organizations to join, and also find faith and work facts.

www.MarketplaceLeaders.org

A website designed to help men and women fulfill their calling in and through the workplace. It includes articles, video, and audio messages to help equip men and women, and free online biblical worker self-assessment. You can sign up for Os Hillman's free daily workplace devotional called "TGIF"—his passion is to equip men and women to see their work as a calling and a ministry. Os says, "I believe we must realize that the workplace is where cultural change is going to take place—through workplace leaders who solve societal problems and gain influence in the strategic spheres to reclaim our culture to the righteousness of Christ."

www.cbmc.com

CBMC (Christian Businessmen's Connection) helps Christian businessmen to connect to other businessmen from all walks of life, and to connect others to Jesus Christ. Offers conferences and resources, including the three-book Operation Timothy discipleship course to take men deeper into the Scriptures in order to deepen their relationship with Christ.

www.fcci.org

Christian business leaders from all industries and professions provide teaching and counsel to members and invited guests at weekly and monthly gatherings and a yearly international conference, as well as through FCCI resources.

www.FaithandWorkResources.com

This website features the best in books, audio, video, and conferences, serving the faith-at-work movement. You can search by categories of interest, product type, or title.

www.maninthemirror.org

Go to the search window and type in "work" for hundreds of free resources, including short, pithy articles, videos, audio recordings, and Bible study materials. Find the "Doing Business God's Way" Bible study series with downloadable group discussion questions available at no cost in video or audio at http://www.maninthemirror.org/biblestudy/series.htm. If you are struggling to find your calling (chapter 1), you can download two free articles, called "Twelve Suggestions to Help Discover Your Calling" and "How to Develop a Written Life Purpose Statement" at www.maninthemirror.org/alm/alm6.htm and www.maninthemirror.org/alm/alm10.htm, respectively.

A MAN'S GUIDE TO THE SPIRITUAL DISCIPLINES

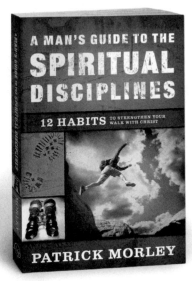

ISBN-13: 978-0-8024-7551-0

For every ten men in church, nine will have children who leave the church. Eight will not find their jobs satisfying. Six will pay only the monthly minimum on their credit card balances. Five will have a major problem with pornography. Four will get divorced (affecting one million children per year). Only one will have a biblical worldview, and all ten will wrestle to balance work and family. With these kinds of issues facing men today, we need more than an annual men's gathering and regular church attendance to keep our faith strong. It takes discipline and determination to stand against the tide. *A Man's Guide to the Spiritual Disciplines* will give men the tools they need to reflect Christ in the context of marriage, family, and the daily grind. And that's what men are made for.

MOODY
PUBLISHERS

1-800-678-8812 . MOODYPUBLISHERS.COM

No Man Left Behind

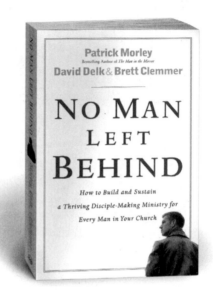

ISBN-13: 978-0-8024-7549-7

David Morrow's book, *Why Men Hate Going to Church*, has heightened awareness of an epidemic—Patrick Morley offers the solution. *No Man Left Behind* is the blueprint for growing a thriving men's ministry that has the power to rebuild the church as we know it, pulling men off the couch and into active involvement as part of the body of Christ.

MOODY
PUBLISHERS

1-800-678-8812 . MOODYPUBLISHERS.COM

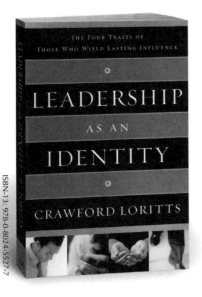

ISBN-13: 978-0-8024-5527-7

LEADERSHIP
AS AN
IDENTITY

Ask yourself this question: What type of character qualifies the people God chooses to use? The question itself assumes an atypical answer, simply because it leaves out so much. To ask only about one's character seems inadequate when defining a leader. We surely need to ask about character, but also about personality, communication skills, IQ, education, previous experience, and more . . . don't we? Crawford Loritts disagrees. He answers the question with four simple words:

BROKENNESS. COMMUNION. SERVANTHOOD. OBEDIENCE.

BROKENNESS.
COMMUNION.
SERVANTHOOD.
OBEDIENCE.

MOODY
PUBLISHERS

1-800-678-8812 . MOODYPUBLISHERS.COM